scrapbooking

Summer 1950

my Mom (right) enjoying a day at the beach with her new sister-in-law, Mary, who is my Dad's sister. They're probably waiting for their loving boys!

Fashion Service

WOMAN'S INSTITUTE MAG

"DRESSMAKER" FASHIONS

French Modes—Millinery—Children's Clothes
How to Make a Georgette Daytime Frock

scrapbooking

Helen Bradley

RONNIE
SELLERS
PRODUCTIONS
PORTLAND, MAINE

First edition published in North America by
Ronnie Sellers Productions, Inc.

P.O. Box 818, Portland, Maine 04104

For ordering information:

(800) 625-3386 toll free

(207) 772-6814 fax

Visit our Web site: www.rsvp.com
• E-mail: rsp@rsvp.com

Ronnie Sellers: President and Publisher
Robin Haywood: Publishing Director
Mary Baldwin: Managing Editor
Charlotte Smith: Assistant Production Editor
Nicole Cyr: Book Editorial Assistant

ISBN 13: 978-1-56906-979-X

ISBN 10: 1-56906-979-4

© The Ilex Press Limited 2007
This book was conceived, designed,
and produced by The Ilex Press Limited,
Cambridge, England

10 9 8 7 6 5 4 3 2 1

Printed and bound in China

All scrapbook layouts supplied by Maya at
www.scrapbookgraphics.com.

contents

Introduction

Scrapbooking in one form or another has been around for hundreds of years as a form of collecting and organizing personal information. In the 1800s women pasted cards, Valentines, and letters into scrapbooks for safekeeping. With the advent of photography, the photo album became common as families collected photographs and fixed them into albums for posterity.

As a child, you may have kept a scrapbook — filling it with writings and items of memorabilia. I filled books full of magazine clippings and personal items and later, as a young woman, I filled more with craft ideas and recipes.

The modern craft of scrapbooking began to take off in the late 1980s when enthusiasts created decorated photo albums that were a combination of scrapbook and photo album. These early scrapbooks had page titles and text recording details about the photos and included elaborate colored paper photo mats, often cut out using decorative scissors. Over time, scrapbookers embraced patterned papers and added embellishments such as stickers, ribbons, fibers, and metal objects as well as die-cut shapes to their pages.

While paper scrapbooking was booming, computer-savvy scrapbookers across the world began to see creative potential in the graphic software they were using. With the advent of digital cameras and the ability to store photos on the computer, it was a short step from paper to digital scrapbooking. Digital scrapbooking has all the elements of paper scrapbooking in a two-dimensional environment and it's just as much fun (if not more) to create!

I've been experimenting with digital crafts since the early days of computers and I've been scrapbooking for the last eight years. It's a fun hobby and it's rewarding to know I'm doing my bit to chronicle my family's history.

I hope that you will enjoy this trip into the world of digital scrapbooking. If you have never scrapped before or if you are a paper scrapbooker looking for new horizons then you'll find everything you need to get started in digital scrapbooking right here.

Helen Bradley

How to use this book

Everything that you need to get started with digital scrapbooking is provided for you right here. Think of the CD as a scrapbooking shop — all the elements, from background papers to embellishments, that you will need to create a scrapbook page are provided for you. In the book you will find help on learning how to use your software to put all the elements together into an attractive layout.

In the first section of this book you will learn how to create a digital scrapbook page using the files provided on the CD and Adobe Photoshop Elements 4. Along the way, you'll learn how to scan images so that you can scan, for example, heritage photos or embellishments of your own. You'll also learn how to print and share your scrapbook pages.

The second section of the book looks at the world of photography and shows you not only how to take better photos, but also how to fix and adjust those photos that you have already taken.

The final section of the book features the templates and art that is available on the CD so that you can plan ahead looking at these pages and find the elements on the CD more easily when you come to create your pages.

I suggest you keep the book open beside you as you work and put your CD in your computer's CD drive so that the scrapbook elements are handy. Launch your Adobe Photoshop Elements software and turn over the page and you're ready to get started with your first digital scrapbook layout.

Planning a scrapbook

You no doubt already have lots of photographs, maybe even hundreds of them, that you plan to scrapbook one day. Sifting through these boxes, or computer folders, full of photos is very daunting. To make the task achievable, make a plan so that the task remains a fun one and not another chore that you need to find time for in your busy day.

Start by giving yourself permission to not scrapbook every photo you have. Pick out the best and most meaningful photos — those that tell the stories that you want to remember.

Determine a theme for your scrapbook. A typical scrapbook will contain anything from 10 to 50 pages so don't expect to fit your life's story into one scrapbook. Instead, determine a theme such as "Johnny's First Years," or "Our trip to Europe" and create one book at a time.

Having a theme automatically narrows down the photos that you need to be concerned with. To begin, copy all the photos that you think you will use to a new folder so that they are easy to find. This also ensures you're working with a copy of the photo and not the original.

Once you have gathered your photos, it's time to look for background papers and embellishments that support your theme. In the final section of this book you will see pictures of the art on the disc — the collection varies from colorful background papers to embellishments such as ribbons and

words. Look through these to get a feel for what is available and what will work with the theme of your book.

The finished templates will give you a starting point for designing your own pages. You can copy these and add your own photos and text to personalize the pages for your book. These finished pages show how the various elements can be assembled together into a page and they're a great place to start when you need some ideas and inspiration.

As you work on your scrapbook, stop every five pages or so and make backup copies of the pages in case of a computer crash. This is also a good time to print the pages, if you haven't already done so.

Once your scrapbook is complete, we'll show you how to print and bind all of the pages into a completed album and give you some ideas for sharing the pages with family and friends.

Remember to take the time to enjoy the creative process and reward yourself for the work that you're doing in chronicling the important parts of your family's history.

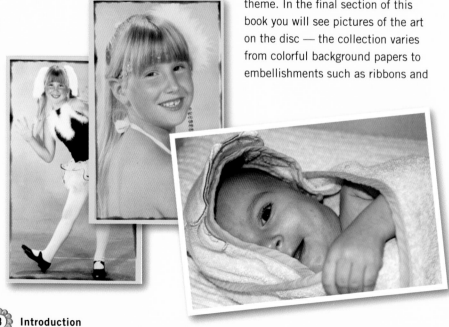

the KEY

My Uncle was destined for a life as a party boy and drinker had it not been his decision to sign up for the Royal Canadian Air Force back in 1950. He was always coming home looking tired with red eyes and my sweet Grandma thought it was because he was working too hard. In 1952 he left for France, the beginning of a life overseas.

and the MAP to a beautiful life

EMPLOYMENT
Help Wanted—Male

FARM HELP—Good teamster and milker, if satisfactory yearly job. Apply R. J. McLachlan, Box 4. Buckingham, Que.

LEARN BARBERING. — The barber trade offers a good living and good business opportunities. All instruction under experienced instructors Vaughn's Barber School Inc., 930 St. Lawrence, Montreal.

POSTAL TAG CARD.

LAC Ronald E. Hicks
RCAF No. 2 Fighter Wing
Grostenquin, France

RuthAnne with her Uncle Ron

September 1952

STYLISH

This leather jacket was a gift that Mommy gave Kyla a few years back, now it's been handed down to Lydia. I think she looks adorable in it, if not a little too grown up. Often when Lydia is playing around dressing up, she asks me if she looks "STYLISH". When she's wearing this cute leather jacket, she most certainly does look STYLISH!

Alysia

Recital June 1985

Invitation to DANCE

Precious

Squeaky Clean B A B Y

Mommy bought this cute Hippo towel on our first real shopping trip in preparation for your homecoming. It's cuddly and soft, and you use it after every bath.

using the templates

contents

Introduction to Photoshop Elements 4

Throughout this book we are using Adobe Photoshop Elements 4 to compile the scrapbook layouts. A 30-day trial version of Photoshop Elements can be downloaded from the Adobe website at www.adobe.com/products/photoshopelwin/tryout.html. If you don't use Photoshop Elements, you should still be able to apply the tips in the book to your own imaging software.

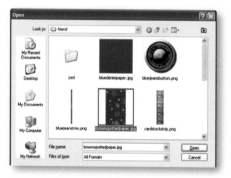

Choosing the right option

When you launch Adobe Photoshop Elements 4 for the first time, you will be given a series of options for what you want to do. Most of the work in this book is done using the *Edit And Enhance Photos* option.

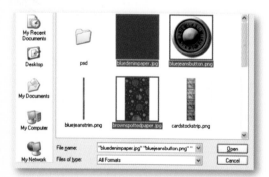

Open multiple images

3 To open multiple images, choose *File > Open* and locate the folder containing the images. Hold the Control (Ctrl) key on your keyboard (or the Command key if you're on a Mac) as you click on each image in turn. When all are selected, click *Open* to open them.

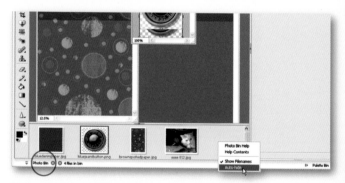

Open a photo

2 To open an image, choose *File > Open* and locate the folder containing the images. Click the *Thumbnails* option in the *View* menu to preview your images. Click the image to open and click the *Open* button.

Using the Photo Bin

4 The *Photo Bin* displays the images you have open. You can display it by clicking the *Photo Bin* link on the *Status Bar* at the foot of the window. If the Photo Bin closes when you move away from it and if you'd like it always open, right/Ctrl-click an empty space on it and disable the *Auto-hide* option.

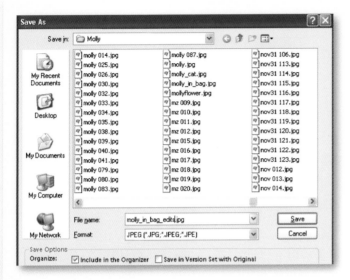

Save a copy of a photo

5 To save a copy of a photo so you won't overwrite the original with the work you're doing, choose *File > Save As* and type a new name for the image. Click the *Save* button.

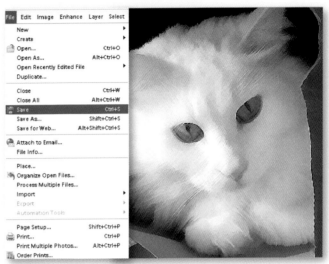

Save your work

6 To save the work that you have done on a photo, choose *File > Save*. Note that this saves the current version of the image, so if you are working on an original, the original will be lost because it will be overwritten with this copy. If you don't want to overwrite the original, perform a *Save As* as detailed in step 5.

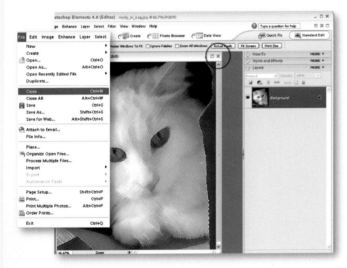

Close an image

7 When you are finished with an image, you can close it. First, save it if desired, then chose *File > Close* to close it. Alternately click the X icon in the top right corner of the image window if you are working on a PC, or the red button in the top left on a Mac.

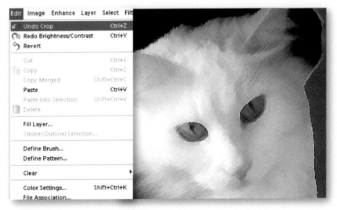

Undo a step

8 To undo a step, such as cropping an image, applying a filter to it, or using a tool to adjust its brightness and contrast, choose *Edit* and click *Undo* (the actual command will read *Undo Crop*, *Undo <filter name>*, *Undo Brightness/ Contrast*, etc., depending on the last command you performed). You can perform the *Undo* task multiple times to roll back changes you have made to your image.

 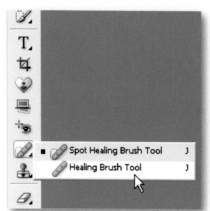

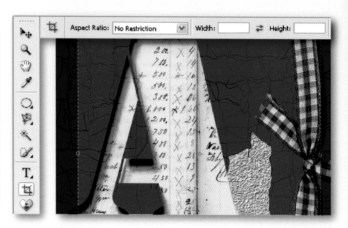

Select a Tool

9 To select a tool to use, click it in the *Tools* palette. If you're unsure what a tool is, hold your mouse over it and a tool tip will appear describing its purpose. Some tool icons have a small black arrow in their bottom-right corner indicating multiple tools sharing the one place on the toolbar. To see the other tools sharing this space, click the arrow to open the fly-out menu. Click any of the tools shown to select it.

Tool Options

10 Whenever you have a tool selected, the *Tool Options Bar* appears just above the image window. It displays important settings that are specific to that tool. Make it a habit to check the *Tool Options Bar* whenever you select a tool, as it offers additional features for fine tuning how the tool works.

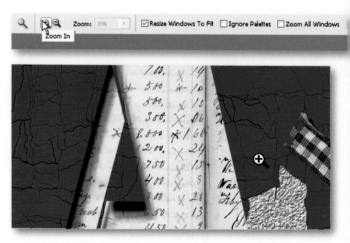

Select Colors

11 To select the foreground and background color to paint with or to use to apply a filter, click the *Foreground Color* box or *Background Color* box at the foot of the *Tools* palette. To reset these to black and white, click the *Default Foreground and Background Colors* button (it shows two squares, one black, one white). To switch the currently selected colors, click the *Switch Foreground and Background Colors* icon (it has a double-headed arrow on it).

Zoom In and Out

12 To zoom in and out of an image, click the *Zoom* tool in the *Tools* palette. Check the *Tool Options Bar* to see if the icon with the plus (+) — *Zoom In* — or the minus (-) — *Zoom Out* — is selected. Click the one you want to use if it isn't selected already, and click on the image to zoom.

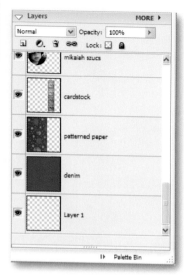

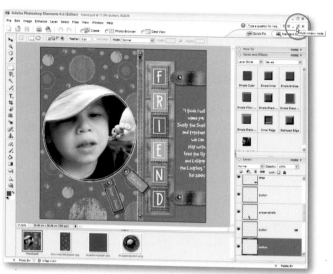

Layers and Styles

13 The *Palette Bin* on the right of the screen contains features such as the *Layers* and *Styles and Effects* palettes. To display and hide the *Palette Bin*, click the *Palette Bin* icon in the bottom right corner of the screen. These palettes can be expanded or contracted by clicking the triangle icon to the left of the palette name.

Sizing windows

14 When you're working with multiple files in Photoshop Elements 4, you will find it easier to move layers from one image to another if you can see the images on the screen. If your screen looks cluttered and you can't see all the images, click the *Multi-Window Mode* button.

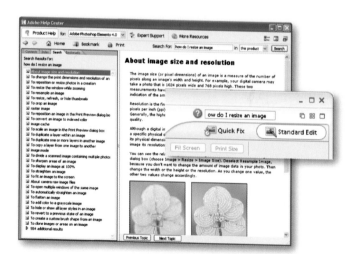

Selecting a brush

15 When you have the *Brush* or *Eraser* tool selected, you can choose a brush shape to use. Click the *Show Selected Brush Presets* drop-down list and choose your brush shape. Soft brushes are generally the best choice because they blend in better than hard brushes. You can set the size of the brush using the slider or use the [and] keys.

Getting Help

16 If there is something you need to do in Photoshop Elements and don't know how, you can get help. Click in the *Help* area in the top right of the window and type a question such as "How do I resize an image," click the question mark icon and the *Product Help* will open, with topics you can click on to get assistance.

Installing fonts

Typefaces, or fonts, are key tools in the creation of a digital scrapbook. You'll use fonts not only for your journaling but also to create wonderful titles for your pages. You'll already have a selection of fonts installed on your computer, but you can find many other fonts free for downloading on the Internet (see Resources, page 96). Before you can use these fonts in your own scrapbook pages, you will need to install them on your PC. Here's how to do just that:

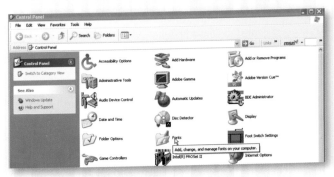

1 On a computer running Windows XP, choose *Start > Control Panel* and click the *Switch to Classic View* link in the top-left corner of the window if it appears there. If there is a link saying *Switch to Category View*, you don't need to change views. Locate the *Fonts* icon and double-click it.

2 Choose *File > Install New Font* and, in the *Drives* area of the dialog, select the drive that contains the font file that you want to install. In the *Folders* area, navigate to the folder containing the font file. When you open this, Windows will display in the *List of Fonts* the names of all the fonts it recognizes in that folder.

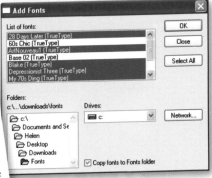

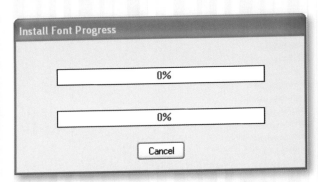

Tip
Many font files that you download from the Internet are zipped or compressed. Before you can install them you have to uncompress them — your computer probably already has software installed to do this. All you need to do is to double-click on the zipped file.

3 Click on the fonts to install. To select multiple fonts, click on the first font, then Ctrl-click on each subsequent font. Click *Select All* if you wish to install all the fonts in the list. Check the *Copy To Fonts Folder* checkbox.

4 Click *OK* and wait as Windows installs the fonts. If a font is already installed on your computer you will get a message indicating this. Simply click *OK* and Windows will continue to install the remaining fonts. When you're done, close the *Fonts* folder. The fonts are now available to all Windows programs and you will find the newly installed fonts in your Photoshop Elements fonts list.

Installing fonts on the Mac

If you're using an Apple Macintosh, fonts are installed in a different way than with Windows. Here's how to do it in Mac OS X.

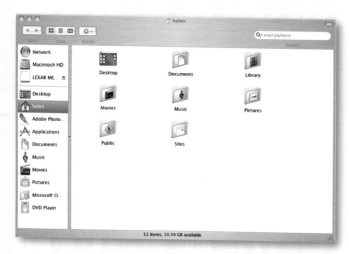

1 Start by closing all open applications — if you don't do this, you may find the fonts will not appear in the font menu of any program that's open while they're being installed.

2 If you are running Mac OS X 10.3 or later, open *Finder* and locate the font file you want to install. Double click the font's icon and the *Font Book* will open, displaying the font so you can check to make sure it's the correct one.

3 If the *Font Book* dialog shows an *Install Font* button, click it to install the font. If the dialog doesn't appear, choose *File > Add Fonts* and click the font to install in the folder display that opens on the screen. Choose to install it *For me only* or *For all users of this computer* and click *Open*.

4 If you are using Mac OS X 10.2 or an earlier version, open a second *Finder* window by choosing *File > New Finder Window*. Click the *Go* menu and click *Home*. Double-click the *Library* folder to open it. Drag and drop the font or fonts to install onto the *Fonts* folder icon in the *Library* folder.

Creating a scrapbook page

It's now time to get started with our first digital scrapbook layout. On the disc are the scrapbook elements you will use to create this first layout. There are also some completed layouts that have been created with these elements and you can use these as inspiration for your own layouts. Over the next few pages we'll create a 12 x 12 inch layout using the Friend series of elements. We'll create the layout step by step so you can see how it is done. We'll also see how to change the color of the final layout to suit the theme.

This is the sample Friend scrapbook page. It is created using two background elements, an image of blue denim and some brown patterned paper. A piece of trim covers the area where these two elements meet. The FRIEND text is patterned paper with the letter piece placed on top. The photo appears inside a circular frame and has two tabs hanging off it, each with words etched into them. On the right of the page are fabric tabs and journaling text. We'll now create our own version of this page, step by step.

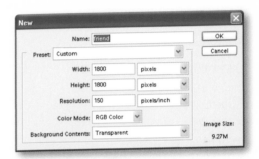

2 Create a new document by choosing *File > New > Blank File*. Set the *Name* to Friend, and set both the *Width* and *Height* to 1,800 pixels. Set the *Resolution* to 150 pixels per inch, the *Background Contents* to *Transparent* and the *Color Mode* to *RGB Color*. Click *OK* to create a new blank document.

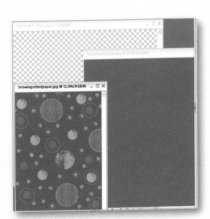

3 Open the first of the images to use by choosing *File > Open* and locate the folder containing the Friends page elements. You will need to open the "friend_blue_denim" and the "friend_brown_spotted" files. Click on the "friend_blue_denim" file, hold the Ctrl/Cmd key, choose the "friend_brown_spotted" file, and click *Open*.

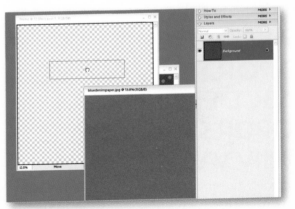

4 Line up the images so that you can see all of them. You may need to drag on the image's title bars to arrange them on the screen. Click on "friend_blue_denim" and, in the *Layers* palette, click on the layer thumbnail for the Background layer to select it. Click and drag the Background layer and drop it into your Friend document.

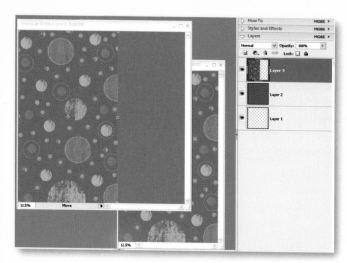

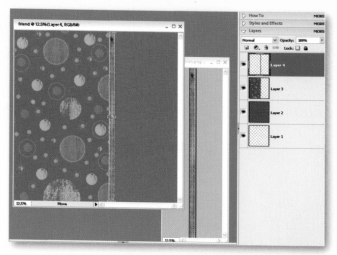

5 Close the "friend_blue_denim" file and click on the "friend_brown_spotted" image. From the *Layers* palette, click and drag the layer thumbnail for the Background layer and drop it onto your Friend document. Click on the Friend document, click on the *Move* tool, then drag the brown spotted paper so it lines up down the left-hand side of the document.

6 Close the "friend_brown_spotted" file and now, from your disc, open these images: "friend_blue_jeans.png" and "friend_button.png." Click the "friend_blue_jeans.png" image to make it current, click on the layer thumbnail for this image in the *Layers* palette and drag and drop it onto your Friend image. Click the *Move* tool and drag the trim until it covers the area where the patterned paper and the blue denim paper meet.

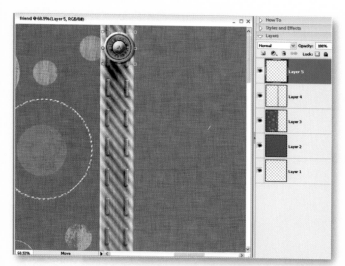

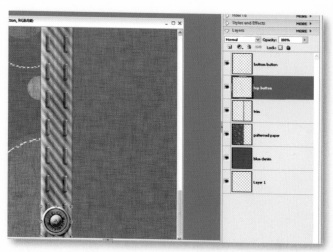

7 Close the "friend_blue_jeans.png" image, and make the "friend_button.png" image current by clicking on its title bar. Click the Background layer thumbnail in the *Layers* palette and drag it onto your Friend image. Using the *Move* tool, move it to the top so it sits over the top of the trim. You may need to zoom into the image to see this area clearly.

8 Repeat step 7, placing the jeans button at the bottom edge of the trim. When you are done, label each layer by double-clicking on the layer name in the *Layers* palette and type a new name describing that layer's contents, which you'll see from the layer's thumbnail image. Close the "friend_button.png" image before proceeding.

Adding a photo

Now you have the background of your first scrapbook page created. It has a piece of brown dotted patterned paper, some denim paper, and some ribbon trim. You're now ready to add a photograph to the page. To do this you'll crop a photograph to a circle shape and add a small frame over the top of it. In a few minutes, you will have the foundation of your page complete.

Tip

Before adding a photograph to your page, make sure you have fixed the photograph so it looks its best. You'll find details of how to do this in the "Improving your photographs" section of the book.

1 Open the photograph that you plan to use for this project by choosing *File > Open*, navigate to the file and open it. Suitable photos might be a friend of yours, your child with a friend, your partner, or even your pet. Because this photograph will be cropped to a circle, make sure you choose one that has plenty of room around the subject so you can cut out your circle.

2 Click on the *Elliptical Marquee* tool (it shares a tool position with the *Rectangular Marquee* tool). Click in the middle of the area of the image to crop to a circle, hold the Shift and Alt/Option keys, and click and drag a circle over the area to use. Release the mouse button and then release the keys. If necessary, drag the circular marquee into position.

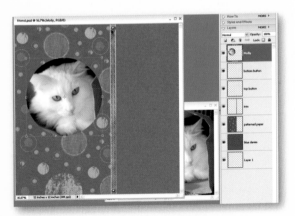

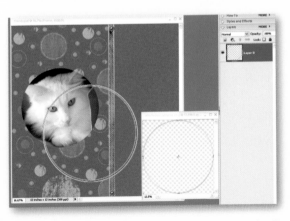

3 Choose *Edit > Copy* to copy the selected area to the clipboard. Click on the Friend image, make sure you have the topmost layer in the *Layers* palette selected and choose *Edit > Paste* and the photo will appear on the page in its own new layer. Name this layer in the *Layers* palette and you can close your photo file.

4 Chances are your image won't be the exact size it needs to be. We'll fix that shortly, for now, let's add the frame so we know how big to make the photo. Open the image "friend_stitched_circle.png" and drag and drop the Background layer containing the frame onto your page. Close the "friend_stitched_circle.png" image and name the frame layer.

Framing a photo

The page we're creating has a circular photo with a framed overlay over it. To make this feature work, we'll need to size and move the photo into position under the frame. In addition, the frame isn't very easy to select, so here's how to do this process as simply as possible.

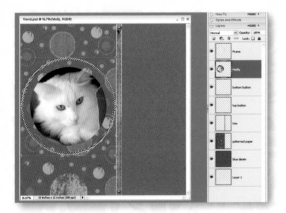

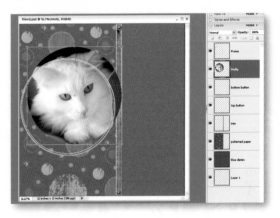

5 Ctrl/Cmd-click on the layer that contains the frame in the *Layers* palette. This selects the frame and you will see the selection marquee with its telltale "marching ants" appear. Click the *Move* tool and drag the frame into position. If the frame seems to 'snap' into position and if you can't move it smoothly, select the *View* menu and choose *Snap to Grid* if it has a checkmark against it so the frame will move smoothly.

6 To turn off the "marching ants", choose *Select > Deselect*. Now click the photo layer in the *Layers* palette to select it. Click the *Move* tool and ensure the *Show Bounding Box* checkbox and the *Auto Select Layer* checkbox on the *Tool Options Bar* are both selected. Hold the Shift key as you drag on one of the corner handles to size the photograph either larger or smaller to fit in the frame. You must use the Shift key or you'll lose the circle shape.

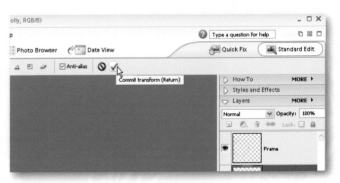

7 Move the photograph into position under the frame and, if necessary, use the sizing handles to size it to the exact size required. If you have difficulty moving small amounts using the mouse when you're moving an object, use the arrow keys on the keyboard to nudge it into position.

8 When you're done, press Enter/Return or click the *Commit Transform* button on the *Tool Options Bar*. You don't have to do this if you're just moving the object, but you do when you resize it.

Adding objects

Tip

If you find it difficult to move an object into a precise position, make sure the View > Snap To Grid option is disabled and try again. If the problem persists, use the Zoom tool to zoom in close to the area you are working on and you will find moving objects much easier.

We are now well underway with our page. We have the background papers in place and our photo cropped to a circle and placed in position. It's time to add the decorative elements to the page, including the title and some tags to jazz it up a bit.

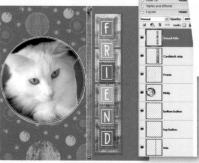

1 For the page title you need two objects—the word "Friend" and the paper element it sits on. Open "friend_strip.png" and "friend_title.png." Select the image "friend_strip.png" and, using the *Layers* palette, click and drag Layer 0 from that file and drop it onto the Friend page. Do the same with the "friend_title.png" image. Close the files "friend_title.png" and "friend_strip.png."

2 Drag the "friend_strip.png" image into position beside the trim and place it approximately equal distance between the top and bottom of the page. Click on the "Friend" wording and drag it into position on top of the cardstock strip. It should be centered approximately inside that strip. Name both layers in the *Layers* palette.

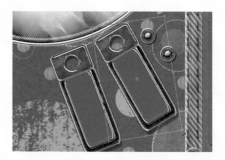

3 To add the tabs on the right-hand side of the page, open the file "friend_strap.png." With this image selected, use the *Layers* palette and drag and drop the strap picture onto your page twice — you need two copies of this image. Close the "friend_strap.png" image and rename your two new layers.

4 Drag each of the strap pictures into position on the right-hand side of the page. They should slightly overlap the strip on which the word "Friend" is written. Open the files "friend_tag.png" and "friend_button.png" and drag and drop two copies of each of the pictures onto your page. Drag the tags into position. To rotate them, select the *Move* tool, click on the tag to select it, and drag on its rotation handle to turn it to the correct angle. Click the *Commit Transform* icon to finish. Repeat for the other tag and then drag the buttons into position on top of the holes in the tags.

Adding shadows

Tip

Shadows work best when you use the same shadow direction for all the objects on the page. You may need to alter the default shadow settings if you have a strong light source in your image. In the image we're using, there is a strong light coming in on the left of the cat's face, so shadows will look best if they fall on the right of objects.

Many of the objects you are working on in this book already have drop shadows provided in the image file. These drop shadows help give each object dimension so that, for example, a sheet of cardstock look as if it has a distinct edge and is layered on top of the background paper instead of being part of it. When you are working with other objects you download from the Internet, for example, some may not have shadows and you will need to add them yourself. Here's how this can be done:

1 Use the *Zoom* tool to zoom into the top of the document where the trim overlays the border between the two papers. The edges of this trim look somewhat flat, so we will add some additional depth using a drop shadow.

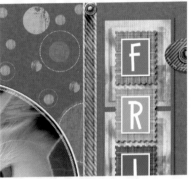

2 Click the trim layer in the *Layers* palette. Open the *Styles and Effects* palette which is above the *Layers* palette. From the first drop-down list, choose *Layer Styles*. From the second list, choose *Drop Shadows*.

3 Apply the *Soft Edge* drop shadow (this and the *Low* shadow are your best choices for most objects). With the drop shadow in place, zoom out to look at the full-size image. If you click the *Undo* and *Redo* buttons you can remove and reapply the shadow to the image and see the difference it makes.

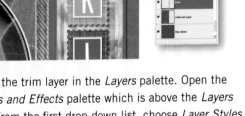

4 To edit the shadow, choose *Layer > Layer Style > Style Settings*. This dialog shows the lighting angle that controls the direction of the light and the distance that the shadow is from the object. You can make adjustments to the angle of the light and size of the shadow in this dialog.

Adding text

One of the most important aspects of scrapbooking is journaling your pages. This is where you write down what is important in the photographs and what it is that the page is trying to convey. We will add two text items to this page, starting with a journaling box that tells the story of why the photo is so important.

1 To ensure the type goes on the topmost layer so it can be seen, click on the topmost layer in the *Layers* palette. From the toolbar, select the *Horizontal Type* tool. Click on the right-hand side of the scrapbook page and drag on it to create a large rectangle between the two tags into which you will type your text. From the *Tool Options Bar*, select a font and font size. We're using a font called "GoodDogPlain" at 24 points in size (this is approximately 8mm high).

2 Click in the *Color* box on the *Tool Options Bar* to select a color — we're using white type. Type some text describing what is happening in the photo.

3 Some fonts, like this one, will not hyphenate correctly because they do not have the required characters in the font file to hyphenate the text properly. If this happens to you, you can change the font by selecting the text and choose another font from the *Font* list. This time I selected Arial Narrow, and it looks fine.

4 An alternative solution is to go through the text and press the Enter key at the end of each line of text. This creates the line breaks manually and bypasses the Photoshop Elements hyphenation feature. Select all the text and click the *Right Align Text* button on the *Tool Options Bar* to make the text line up against the right-hand side of the page.

Advanced text options

The tags below the frame are a place that we can use to add some extra text. In the sample layout, the tags have words describing the child in the photo. I'll use the tags for the cat's name and the date the photo was taken. In this page, you'll see how to put text on an object like these tags and how to give it an attractive raised appearance.

1 Use the *Zoom* tool to zoom into the area of the image that you will be working on. Click the *Horizontal Type* tool, select your font, font color, and font size, and click anywhere on the image (don't draw a rectangle this time, just click once). Type the word to put on the first tag and click the *Commit any current edits* icon on the *Tool Options Bar*.

2 Click the *Move* tool and click on the text. Drag the text into position over the tag. Hover your mouse pointer over one of the corner handles until it shows a double-headed curved arrow and then drag a corner to rotate the text into position on the tag. Drag the corners to size the text to fit the tag. Click the *Commit Transform* icon on the *Tool Options Bar*.

3 Display the *Styles and Effects* palette and choose *Layer Styles > Drop Shadows*. With the text layer still selected, apply a *Soft Edge* drop shadow to the layer. Choose *Layer Styles > Bevels* and apply a *Simple Sharp Inner* bevel.

4 Repeat steps 1 and 2 to add text to the second tag. This time, right/Ctrl-click the first text layer with its style in the *Layers* palette and choose *Copy Layer Style*. Now click on the new text layer that does not yet have the style attached to it. Right/Ctrl-click and choose *Paste Layer Style* to paste the style and save having to apply it manually.

Scanning an image

When you want to create a digital scrapbook page using a physical photo, you'll need to convert the photo to a graphic file by scanning it. You can do the same thing if you want to use an item of memorabilia, such as a ticket, school report, or certificate. Here's how to scan a photo or other item and a tip for what to do if you don't have a scanner.

1 Make sure the scanner glass is clean and, if there is a chance that the item to be scanned might scratch the scanner glass, place a sheet of thin transparent plastic over the scanner glass to protect it. Place the item to be scanned on the flat bed of your scanner.

2 If you are using Windows XP you have two choices of software. You can use the *Scanner and Camera Wizard* or your scanner's own software. To launch the Wizard, choose *Start > All Programs > Accessories > Scanner and Camera Wizard*. If you prefer, launch your scanner's own software — you will find the scanning process is very similar. If the *Scanner and Camera Wizard* detects multiple devices attached to your computer, you will be prompted with "Which device do you want to use?". Select your scanner from the list and click *OK*. When the *Scanner and Camera Wizard* dialog appears, click *Next*.

3 Click the *Preview* button to view the image in the preview area. You can then drag the handles around the image — there's no point to scanning any more of the image than you need to, and, in fact, it can make for very large files if you try to do this. Select the type of image, generally *Grayscale picture* or *Color picture* are best (don't use *Black and white picture or text* for black and white photos, use *Grayscale* instead).

4 Click the *Custom settings* button to configure the scanning resolution. It is generally not advisable to adjust *Brightness* and *Contrast* at this stage, as you can't see the result on the your image — it's best to do this later in your graphics software. However, you can set the resolution, as this can't be done later.

Scanning resolution

When you scan an image, you need to make a choice of how much detail to scan. To do this, you need to determine whether you will use the image at its original size or smaller or larger. While you might think you should just scan at a very big size, this isn't always a good idea because the file size can be very large, so your disk will fill up very quickly.

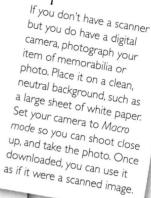

Tip

If you don't have a scanner but you do have a digital camera, photograph your item of memorabilia or photo. Place it on a clean, neutral background, such as a large sheet of white paper. Set your camera to *Macro* mode so you can shoot close up, and take the photo. Once downloaded, you can use it as if it were a scanned image.

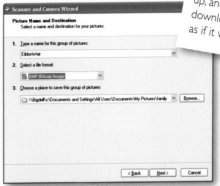

5 The default scanning resolution of 150dpi is a good resolution for printing the image on your layout. This is because the layouts on the CD accompanying this book are provided at 150dpi. To print the photo at half its original size, scan the image at 75dpi. Scan at 300dpi if you want to use the image at a larger size.

6 Click the *Preview* button again to preview the image with your new settings — if you vary the resolution you won't see any changes but other settings will alter the preview. When all is ready to go, click *Next*. Type a name for your image and choose a folder to place it in. If necessary, click *Browse* to select the folder to use. Choose a format for the image from the list, all are suitable.

7 Click *Next* and wait as the scanner scans the image. When the scan is complete the *Other Options* dialog will appear — click *Next* to continue. When the final step in the Wizard appears, you can click the link on the page to open the folder that contains the scanned image.

8 With the dialog containing the scanned image on the screen, you can drag and drop the scanned image into Photoshop Elements. From here you can make any corrections to the image, and you can then use it in your layouts in the same way as you would use any image downloaded from your camera.

Cropping an image

Whether you are using an image you've downloaded from your camera or one that you have scanned, chances are you may need to crop it to make it look its best and so it fits well with the layout you've chosen. Here's how to crop an image in Photoshop Elements.

1 This is a pleasant enough image, but it's somewhat marred by the clutter of furniture behind the subject and the distracting elements on her clothes. It will benefit from these distractions being removed or at least minimized.

2 Click the *Crop* tool on the *Tools* palette and click and drag a crop marquee onto the image. Notice how the area that is outside the crop marquee is darkened so you can see more clearly the portion of the image that will be left when you finish cropping.

3 Drag on the handles of the marquee and experiment with different ways of cropping the image. Notice that you can crop very close — even cropping away the top of the child's head — and it will still look fine. When you have a crop you like, click the *Commit current crop operation* icon (the checkmark one) under the crop marquee, or double click on the photo to complete the crop.

Tip

There is no right or wrong way to crop a photo. Experiment with your images and see how you can improve them by cropping. Try and get in close to what you think is important in the photo — you can always *Undo* it if you don't like the result.

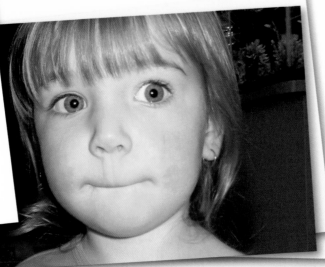

4 You might be surprised by the final choice of crop for this photo. The photo has changed from one which is tall to one which is wide, and the focus is clearly on the subject's funny expression. Compare it with the original — this one will look much more exciting on a scrapbook layout.

Scaling and rotating images

When you're working with digital photos you will sometimes need to prepare an image to a fixed size. For example, you might want to size or crop a series of images to the same dimensions to use on a layout. Here's how to scale your images to a preset size.

I This photo has been cropped fairly heavily from the original image. Right now, I'm not only unsure how big it is, but I also want to size it so it will fit on a 12 x 12 layout. I have determined I need it to be 8 inches tall.

2 To check the image's size and to resize it to the required size, choose *Image* from the menu and then choose *Resize > Image Size*. The dialog shows you the current dimensions of the image (approximately 21 x 27 inches) and its resolution (72 pixels per inch).

3 Set the resolution to 150 pixels per inch to match the resolution of your layout. When you do this, the image width and height will also be reduced. Check the *Resample Image* checkbox and set the *Resample Image* mode to *Bicubic Smoother*. Check the *Constrain Proportions* checkbox and set the *Height* to the desired value (the *Width* is adjusted automatically). Click *OK*.

Tip

The *Constrain Proportions* checkbox, when enabled, ensures that the image is scaled up in proportion and not skewed out of shape. You should always enable this checkbox and then set either the desired *Width* or *Height* value and let Photoshop Elements calculate the other dimension.

4 You probably won't see much difference on screen, but this image is now exactly 8 inches high so it will be the perfect size for my layout.

Having fun with objects

You have a wonderful collection of scrapbook papers and objects on the disc that you can use to create your scrapbook pages. You can mix and match these on your pages and you can adjust how each item looks to suit each page. Here are some great tricks and tips for getting the maximum benefit from the disc objects.

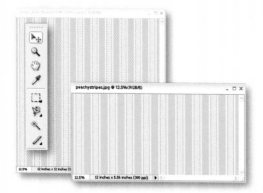

Stretch to fit

1 Here, we've used the "cutie_patootie_peachy_stripes.png" paper as a background paper even though it is smaller than the page. After you've dropped the image into the document, click the *Move* tool and drag on the sizing handles to stretch the paper to fill the page. You can't successfully stretch all images out of shape this way, but many work just fine.

Duplicate to fit

2 When an image won't stretch to fit an area, you can copy it multiple times and then arrange the pieces on the page to fit. Here two copies of "just_us_aged_writing.png" are placed on the page and the "just_us_ribbon_bow.png" image is used to cover the area where they meet. Tuck a photo behind the ribbon and you have a wonderful page background.

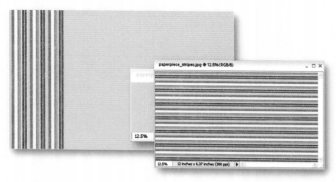

Rotate to fit

3 Some striped papers will look wonderful if they're rotated to the opposite direction. Here I've used the "lickety_stripes.png" paper once and multiple copies of the "lickety_blue_textured.png" image. Both papers are added and then rotated and moved into position.

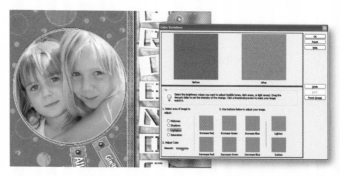

Recolor

4 If an object isn't the right color for your layout, you can easily change it. Click the layer and choose *Enhance > Adjust Color > Color Variations*. You can then choose to add or remove colors from the *Variations* dialog. Do this for the *Midtones*, *Shadows*, and *Highlights* then click *OK*.

Rewrite the words

5 If the words on a tag or another element don't work for your layout, you can change them. Use the *Clone Stamp* tool (see page 46) to sample a piece of the image that doesn't have text on it and that is a good match for the area that the text is on. Paint out the text with the *Brush* tool, then add a new text layer to your layout with the words of your choice. Add a shadow or bevel to the text to finish.

Cut off pieces

6 When an object like a ribbon, bookplate, or bow has more detail than you need or is too long, you can often cut off the piece you don't want. Open the image and, before you place it on your layout, make a selection using the *Rectangular Marquee* tool to select only the area you want to use and choose *Edit > Copy*. Select your layout image and choose *Edit > Paste* to paste the cropped item onto a new layer.

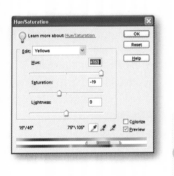

Multiple recoloring

7 You can recolor a multicolored item by using *Enhance > Adjust Color > Adjust Hue/Saturation*. Choose the color to alter from the *Edit* list, and adjust it using the *Hue* slider. Adjust the *Saturation* and *Lightness* to tweak the look. You won't be able to control the colors accurately, but you should be able to achieve a better color scheme for your project.

Make new objects

8 With a few simple steps you can create objects that didn't exist before. Striped paper can be cut into a narrow strip to make ribbon — add a small drop shadow to it so it looks three-dimensional. Drag and drop one flower image twice onto the page and size one a little smaller than the other. Recolor one if desired, and so on.

There is a world of opportunity in the images you have on the disc — enjoy them and tweak them to enhance your pages.

Printing your page

Now you have finished creating your first scrapbook page, you'll be anxious to print it so you can show everyone. To print the finished page, you will need a color printer and some suitable paper. I like to use high quality matte photo paper that is compatible with my printer — the printed page has a wonderful texture and the ink is very stable, so the page can be handled without damage. You can also use the regular white cardstock used for scrapbook pages.

Tip

If your printer won't print full size 12 x 12, it's easy to resize the pages to fit. See the instructions on page 29 for scaling images, or select the *Print Size > Fit on Page* option from the *Print Preview* dialog to have Elements automatically resize the image before printing.

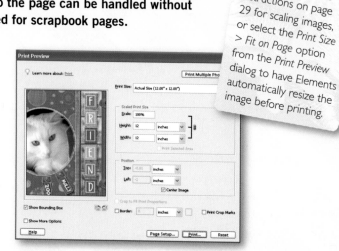

1 Before you print your page, save it to your hard drive so you have a copy stored if you encounter problems printing it and so you can make adjustments if it doesn't print as expected. To do this, choose *File > Save As* and type a name for the page. From the *Format* list choose *Photoshop (*.PSD,*.PDD)* and locate the folder in which to save the page. Click *Save*.

2 To print the page, choose *File > Print*. This opens the *Print* dialog, which shows a preview of your image and details about how it is set to print — all these options can be configured to suit your needs.

3 To set the page size to match the paper you will be using in your printer, click the *Page Setup* button. From the *Size* list, choose the size of the paper you will be using — I use 13 x 19 paper to print 12 x 12 on my printer because it can't print borderless on 12 x 12 paper. Choose the size that matches your paper size and click *OK*.

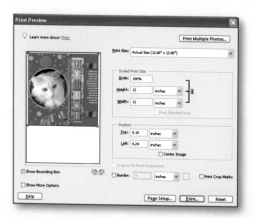

4 Use the *Scaled Print Size* area to size the image, and, if required, disable the *Center Image* checkbox so you can position the image where you want it to appear on the paper. Here, I've moved it to the top of the paper so there is less waste.

Advanced printing options

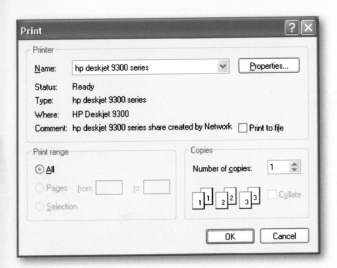

5 When you're ready to print, click the *Print* button. This displays a *Print* dialog. It's now time to configure your printer for the paper type you're using, so click *Properties* to open the *Properties* dialog.

6 What you see now on your screen depends on the printer you are using. All printers are different, but the basics are similar. Start by finding an option for telling the printer the type of paper you're using.

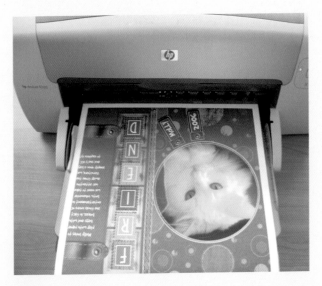

7 Once you've selected the paper, you will see options for the quality that can be achieved with that paper. Select your desired *Print Quality*. *Normal* quality works well for most pages — it is economical on ink, and printing is faster than choosing *Best* quality.

8 When you're ready, press *Print* to print your page. It may take a while for a large job such as this to print, so allow it plenty of time. When the print job is complete, remove the paper from the printer and set it aside until the ink is dry before handling the page.

Binding your scrapbook

In time, as you work on your scrapbook, you will have a stack of printed pages. So what to do with them now? Assembling them into an album is a good way to make them accessible so you can enjoy them, and also to protect them so they won't get damaged. Here are some album and display ideas, both traditional and not so traditional!

1 Purchase your album before you start printing your pages because you'll need to make sure you're printing the pages at the right size for the album you're using. The pages we've been making so far in this book are all square and designed for a 12 x 12 in album.

2 Once you have printed your pages, use a sharp pair of scissors or a paper trimmer to trim them to the right size and to remove any of the white paper around the printed area where the printer won't print. Make sure the pages are straight and neat.

3 Most albums you purchase from a scrapbooking store are ideal for digital scrapping, as they contain plastic page protectors to hold the pages. You simply slip the page into the plastic insert. If you're making digital layouts, you can fit quite a lot of pages into your album so buy extra packs of page protectors when you buy the album.

Tip
If your paper trimmer or scissors are chewing up the edges of your paper rather than cutting through them, it's time to invest in a new blade for the trimmer or a new pair of scissors.

4 When you're assembling your album, consider the story you are telling. If you are chronicling family life, place photos when the kids are younger in the front pages and move to photos of them more grown up later in the album. If you're telling the story of an overseas trip, start with the earlier part of the trip and move on through your travels. If you haven't yet made pages for all your photos, leave empty spaces where these pages will ultimately go.

Other display options

I love my full-size 12 x 12 albums but they don't fit into a handbag very easily. So I like to make mini albums using my digital designs in addition to larger albums. Mini albums are great because they are portable so I can take them with me just about anywhere. They can be handed around and enjoyed, and they're small enough for me to display one on my desk at work and still have room for my French Press! This is one clear benefit of digital scrapping over paper scrapping: you can print one page as many times as you like to create many albums from it.

Tip

If your album pages are not square, create a page in Photoshop Elements the size of the album page and at 150 ppi resolution. Create your layout in this document just as you would any square scrapbook page.

5 The design of a typical mini album often doesn't allow you to add extra pages and it often does not have page protectors. These albums can be used for small projects, such as favorite photos from vacation, photos of a pet, or as a gift for family and friends. These albums are small — often smaller than 6 x 6 in — and you'll find them at any scrapbook store.

6 Accordion-style mini albums are great to use, as they open to display a series of pages at once. Make sure to trim your printed pages to a little smaller than the album page, and use glue to stick the photos in. These albums don't have page protectors, so you want the pages to stay where they are and to survive some rough handling — they're made to be enjoyed.

7 Other solutions for your pages include using shallow tins such as you might receive in the mail containing promotional CDs. Pages can be joined together daisy-chain-style on a ribbon so they pull out for display, or simply cropped and stored in the tin for viewing and sharing. In this situation, you can use a corner rounder that you can purchase from a scrapbook store to round the corners of the pages so they fit better.

8 When you're making albums of photos, don't overlook other ways to enjoy your pages. One method is to place photos into frames to display around the house. You will find 12 x 12 in and square frames in other sizes at framing stores, and some albums have covers that will take a photo for display purposes. Even recycled CD jewel cases can be put into service as a display frame.

E-mailing a page

Scrapbook pages are perfect for sharing with friends and family. It's not always convenient or appropriate to make a printed copy and sometimes it's easier to share a layout in an informal way, such as e-mailing it. The most important thing to consider when e-mailing is file size. Large files take a long time to send and receive, and many mailboxes have limits on the size of files they can receive. Here's how to e-mail a page.

Tip

As a rule of thumb most people's monitors are 1280 × 1024 pixels in size. If you send a photo larger than this, it will be too big to display. An image 450 × 450 pixels in size will display at approximately 6 × 6 inches on the screen — that's a good size to aim for.

1 This finished page is ready to e-mail to a friend or family member. However, right now it weighs in at over 120MB. It could take an hour or more to send it, and the recipient might not even receive it because it's so big, and it will take days to download it on a dialup connection.

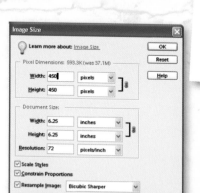

2 Choose *Image > Resize > Image Size* and check the *Constrain Proportions* and *Resample Image* checkboxes and set *Mode* to *Bicubic Sharper*. Set the *Resolution* to 72 pixels per inch and set the *Width* to 450 pixels. Click *OK* and wait as the image is sized down. Now it's an ideal size to e-mail.

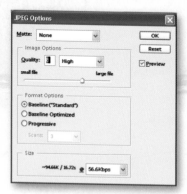

3 Save the file by choosing *File > Save As* and type a name for the file. From the *Format* list choose *JPEG (*.JPG, *.JPEG, *.JPE)* and choose a folder to store the file in. Click *Save* and when the *JPEG Options* dialog appears, choose *High* from the *Quality* list and click *OK*. This saves the file in a format that most people can view, and at a fairly small file size.

4 Launch your e-mail software, write the e-mail, and attach the image as you would normally. You can also e-mail a page from inside Photoshop Elements. Choose *File > Attach to E-mail* and follow the step-by-step instructions.

Sharing on the Web

Do you have your own Web site? Many digital scrappers do, and putting your pages on the Web lets you share them with a worldwide audience. That's not the only method available to you — to share your pages you can publish them to your blog, put them on a photo site, or upload them to a scrapbook gallery. Whichever option you choose, size your image as if you were going to e-mail it, using the instructions on the previous page, before you start. Here are some ideas for sharing your pages.

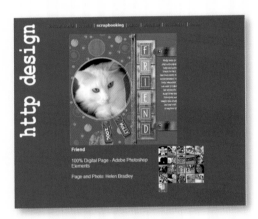

1 If you have your own Web site, you can publish any page you like to it. Explaining how to create a Web site is beyond the scope of this book, but if you already have a site, you'll know how it's done. The Photoshop Elements Organizer also has a *Create* tool you can use to create an HTML photo gallery.

2 If you have a blog, you can include the scrapbook page on it. Visit your blog site and create a new blog entry. Type the text for your blog entry, and insert your photo. When you're done, publish your post. Anyone reading your blog will be able to see and enjoy your page.

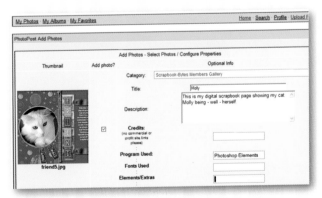

3 A site like Flickr.com is designed for sharing photos and it's a great place for sharing your scrapbook pages, too. You will need to sign up for Flickr, as with most photo sites (there are lots on the Web and many, like Flickr, are free), and then you can upload your photos with a few mouse clicks.

4 Many online scrapbooking communities have galleries where you can upload your pages to share with others. For example, Scrapbook-bytes.com has a very active community. Uploading a page is very simple and within minutes the page is there for all the world to see and to comment on.

Making a slide show

Digital scrapbook pages lend themselves to being shared and viewed electronically. One way to do this is to create a slide show. Once you have done this, you can play it on your computer any time. You can also burn the show, complete with narration and music, to a VCD (video CD) or DVD so it can be played and viewed in almost any home DVD player.

Tip
To save your finished slide show to your hard drive so you can play it on your computer, click Output, choose Save as a File, choose the Movie File (.wmv) option and click OK. Type a name for your slide show file and click Save.

1 Launch the *Organizer* tool in Photoshop Elements and click on one of the pages to include in your slide show — you only need to select one for now. Click the *Create* button on the top of the window. When the *Creation Setup* dialog appears, click *Slide Show* and click *OK*.

2 Set the options for the slide show, such as how long a page will display for and the type of transition to use. Also set the *Quality* of the show. To protect your pages from being cropped don't select either cropping option. Click *OK* to continue to the next step.

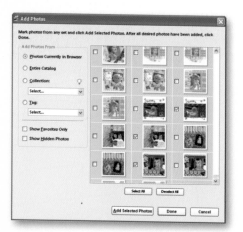

3 Click the *Add Media* button and choose *Photos and Videos from Folder* or *Photos and Video from Organizer*, depending on whether your files are in the *Organizer* or simply stored in a folder. If they are in a folder, select the page images to include and click *Open*. If they are in the *Organizer*, click those to add and click *Add Selected Photos* and then click *Done*.

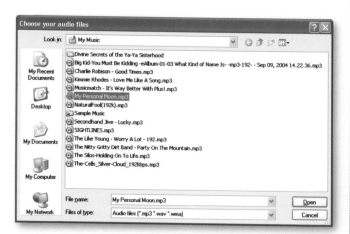

4 If you have music stored on your computer you can make it play as the slide show plays. To add music, choose *Add Media* and then *Audio from Folder* and browse and locate a track to use. You will see the track appear along the foot of the slide show window.

Burning a VCD or DVD

Tip

If you do not have Adobe Premiere Elements, you may have another DVD-writing program on your computer — often these are provided with the computer you buy. Check your program list or the manuals that came with your computer to see what you have installed.

Now you've created your slide show it's time to decide what to do with it. One option is to write it to a disc, such as a VCD (video CD) or DVD. To make a DVD you will need a DVD writer, and to make a VCD you will need a CD writer. If you have Adobe Photoshop Elements with Premiere Elements, you have the right software to do both. Here's how to create a DVD.

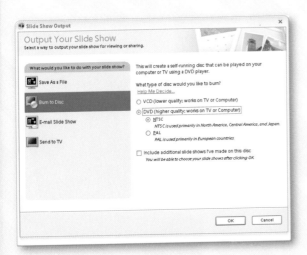

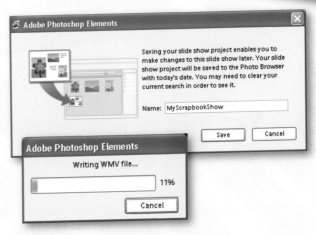

1 With the *Slide Show Editor* visible on the screen, click the *Output* button, choose *Burn to Disc*, and then choose the *DVD* option. Choose *NTSC* or *PAL* as the format, depending on what country you live in, and Click *OK* to continue.

2 When you are prompted to save the slide show project, click *OK* and then type a name for your project and click *Save*. Type a name for the WMV (Windows Media Video) movie file and click *Save* again. Wait as the file is written to disc.

3 In Premiere Elements, type a name for your project and click *OK*. When the main screen opens, your movie will be in place on the screen. If you only have one movie, select the *Auto-play DVD with no Menus* option and click *OK* to continue.

4 Click *Preview DVD* to preview the movie. When you're ready to continue, click *Burn DVD*. When the *Burn DVD* dialog opens, select your DVD drive and configure any other settings. When you're done, test the disc in your DVD player.

improving your photographs

contents

How to take better photos

One side benefit of the popularity of digital cameras is that most of us are taking more and better photographs than ever before. The immediate feedback you get by being able to see the photos in your camera just after you take them lets you assess the quality of the shot and take another if it's not what you want. Here are some ways you can improve the photos you take.

Get in close

One of the quickest ways to improve your photographs is to take a step or two (or more!) toward your subject. Allowing your subject to fill the viewfinder not only gives you more of the subject in your photograph, but also reduces the impact of untidy backgrounds.

Use your flash

You might not think you need a flash on a sunny day, but your portraits will be better if you do. Use the flash to light the subject's face so it is not hidden in shadow. You should also use a flash when photographing a person in front of a landscape, waterfall, or beach scene to light them properly.

Better close-ups

Most digital cameras have a macro setting, which is indicated by a small flower icon on the camera. Use this instead of the zoom when shooting flowers, babies, and even pets close up.

Filtering reflected light

If you own a digital SLR camera, consider purchasing a polarizing filter for it. Use it on bright sunny days to get more saturated colors in your photos.

Check the background

Before you take any photograph, check what's in the background — if you're using a point-and-shoot camera, check the LCD screen because this gives the best representation of what you're about to capture. Often moving a step or two to the right or left removes distracting elements to give a better photograph.

Capture speed

When photographing small, active children, pets, or moving objects, use the sports mode on your camera. This mode helps freeze the action so you won't get so many blurry shots. Also, try moving the camera with the motion to get a still subject with a pleasantly blurry background.

Frame your shot

Use your camera's viewfinder to frame your photo. Mentally divide the photo area using two horizontal and two vertical lines (like a tic-tac-toe board) and position objects of interest along the lines or where they intersect. This, for example, ensures a horizon never runs across the middle of the photo.

Room to move

When photographing a moving object or one that suggests movement, such as a bike or car, capture an area in front of the object so that it feels like there's room for it to travel forward. Cutting off the back is preferable to cutting off the front.

Jargon Buster

SLR
Single Lens Reflex — these cameras generally have interchangeable lenses, and when you line up the picture you preview it through the same lens that takes the photo. This gives you better control over framing the photo and focusing it.

Polarizing filter
A round glass filter that screws onto a camera lens or sits in a special filter rack in front of the lens. The filter reduces reflections and glare so skies are darker. The filter's effect can be adjusted by rotating it.

LCD
Liquid Crystal Display — a small screen on the back of a digital camera that you can use to frame your photos and to view a photo when you have taken it. In general, the LCD screen is a better choice for previewing a photo than using the viewfinder.

Fixing red eye

Red eye occurs when you take a photograph using the camera's flash at night or indoors. It is evidenced by a person's pupils showing as red instead of black, and it can spoil an otherwise lovely photo. In many cases it's unavoidable, but luckily Photoshop Elements has all the tools you need to fix the problem.

I This photo was taken indoors in low light conditions with a flash. The result is a pretty portrait that's marred by the fact that both eyes are unnaturally red. The photo needs fixing.

2 With your image open in Photoshop Elements, click the *Red Eye Removal* tool in the Toolbar. Notice that the cursor changes to a crosshair shape. Click on the first problem eye to fix it.

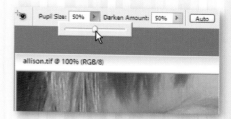

3 If the fixed area is too small or too large, adjust the *Pupil Size* value in the *Tool Options Bar*. Increase the *Pupil Size* percentage to make the area bigger and reduce the percentage to make it smaller.

If desired, increase the *Darken Amount* to darken the area more and decrease it to make it less dark.

Tip

When the **Red Eye Removal** tool is selected you can click the **Auto** button on the **Tool Options Bar** and Photoshop Elements will attempt to locate and fix the red eye problem automatically. This isn't always successful, and if not, you will need to use the procedure outlined here.

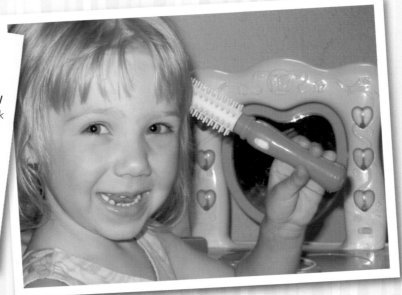

4 Here, we have fixed both eyes and, as you can see, the photo looks much better than it did previously.

Removing skin blemishes

Tip

The *Spot Healing Brush* tool is handy for fixing problems other than skin blemishes. It can be used to fix damage to heritage photos after you have scanned them and to remove very small unwanted objects in photos.

In an ideal world, everyone's skin would be smooth and flawless and no one would ever have a scratched knee or an unwanted pimple. Unfortunately, we don't live in such a Utopia, but Photoshop Elements can help to fix all sorts of skin blemishes in your photos.

This is a cute photo of a young girl sporting her favorite sunglasses, but a scratch on her knee detracts from the image. We can fix this problem in Elements to make her skin blemish free.

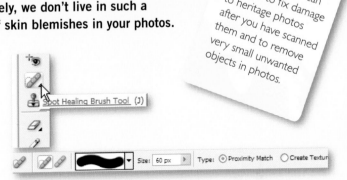

2 With the image open in Photoshop Elements, locate and click the *Spot Healing Brush* on the Toolbar — it shares a position with the *Healing Brush* tool. Select a brush shape from the drop-down brush list, a soft round brush is a good choice. Adjust the size of the brush so that it just covers the blemish.

3 Click once on the blemish to remove it. If you don't like the result, click the *Undo* button on the Toolbar and try again.

If you have more than one blemish, fix them one at a time by clicking on each in turn. Remember to adjust the brush size each time so that it just covers the blemish.

4 With the injury on her knee fixed, this portrait is now ready for scrapping.

Fixing larger problems

Sometimes you will capture a photo with a pole, electrical wire, or sign in the background. These elements can ruin a photo because your eye is drawn to them. Removing the distraction will make the photo more attractive and will make the subject of the photo, and not the unwanted object, the main focus of the picture.

1 This is a lovely photo of three girls by some falls. All the colors in the photo are blue or neutral giving the photo a muted color palette. This effect is somewhat ruined by the red danger sign, which is out of place in this rural setting. The photo will look much better without the sign in it.

2 Select the *Clone Stamp* tool on the toolbar. Hold the Alt/Option key, and click on an area of the image that will be used to paint out the object. Choose an area that will blend into the surrounding image.

Choose a soft round brush from the *Brush* drop-down list and size it large enough to fix a good size piece of the problem with each click, but not so large that you'll cover over areas that you want to keep.

3 Click with the mouse over the problem area to paint it out — clicking generally works better than painting. As you click, the paintbrush paints out the object, replacing it with the sampled image.

If necessary, you can sample another part of the image using Alt/Option-click and continue to paint until the object is painted out. If you need to make the brush smaller or larger press the [or] keys as required.

Tip

You'll get best results with the *Clone Stamp* tool if you click repeatedly, rather than painting with long strokes.

Be patient, cloning is seldom a one-click fix and it can take some time to get a good result. Work slowly and take a new sample whenever you need to alter the color you're painting with. Adjust the size of the brush as you work so you don't paint over areas that don't need fixing.

4 Here is the fixed image — now the sign is gone the image looks much better. It took a few minutes to complete the process of removing the sign, but the result was worth the effort.

Improving an image

Sometimes you'll look at a photograph and, even if you don't understand what is wrong with it, you'll think it's lackluster. You will see that the colors are more gray and muddy than you recall the scene to have been. The image needs brightening and some general improvement and Photoshop Elements has a tool for this.

1 This image shot from across a valley is a pleasant enough image, but it lacks brightness and clarity. The tones in the image tend to be a neutral gray; there are not a lot of areas with dark black color. What color there is, is muddy and dull. It needs a boost.

2 To fix the image, select the *Enhance* menu and click *Auto Smart Fix*. Photoshop Elements automatically processes the image and corrects its color balance. It also improves the shadow and highlight detail if this is required and it does all of this with no input from you.

3 If the fix that is applied using the *Auto Smart Fix* tool is not sufficient, you can increase the intensity of the fix by clicking the *Enhance* menu and choosing *Adjust Smart Fix*. Increase the amount of the fix up to 200 percent of the original. Click the *Preview* checkbox to see the result of the fix on your image.

Tip

If the *Auto Smart Fix* tool does not work for your image, click the **Undo** button and, instead, try the individual levels, contrast, or color correction fixes. You can find these by clicking the **Enhance** menu. Choose **Auto Levels** to adjust the image contrast, but take care as this tool may alter the colors in the image.

4 This image looks vastly different to the original. The *Auto Smart Fix* tool has brought back the color and vibrancy of the scene, and it's a photograph that we can now scrap with pride.

Recovering detail from shadows

It's not unusual when you photograph a person in front of a landscape that you get a photo with a wonderful background but with the person in the foreground in deep shadow. If you've read the photography tips section you'll know you can avoid this by using your camera's flash or fill flash when shooting in daylight conditions. If you've taken the photo already, here's how to fix the problem.

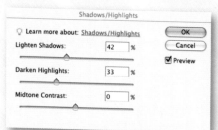

1 This photograph, taken on vacation in England, has a nicely lit background but the woman in the foreground is in shadow and we can't see her face clearly. We'll fix it so that we can see both her and the lovely building behind her.

2 Choose *Enhance > Adjust Lighting > Shadows/Highlights* to display the *Shadows/Highlights* dialog. Check the *Preview* checkbox so you can see the results, and adjust the *Lighten Shadows* slider until you can see the features on the person in the foreground.

3 Adjust the *Darken Highlights* slider if necessary to bring some detail back in the lighter areas of the image. You can also adjust the *Midtone Contrast* slider if desired to bring contrast back in the middle tones in the image. If the tones look OK, leave the slider at 0.

4 As you can see, this relatively simple adjustment has brought back the detail in the woman's face without destroying the detail of the building in the background. You should try to remember to use the fill flash when taking pictures like this, but the *Shadows/Highlights* tool can help in an emergency.

Fixing skin tones

Often when you take a photo of a person close up you will find that their skin tones look unnatural in the final photo. This can occur because the camera's light balancing function doesn't accurately adjust for the type of light you're shooting in. Luckily, Photoshop Elements has a very smart fixing tool to help you make skin tones look more natural.

Tip

Light has many different hues. It is a different color in the early morning and early evening than it is at midday. Indoors, light bulbs cast a yellow/orange color on your photos and fluorescent light throws a green/blue cast. An automatic camera will try to adjust for the differences but it doesn't always get it right.

1 This photo of three youngsters showing off their braces was taken inside, and the camera has not adjusted correctly to the light, with the result that the image and, in particular, their skin color is tinged with blue. This can easily be fixed in Photoshop Elements.

2 Click the *Enhance* menu and choose *Adjust Color > Adjust Color for Skin Tone* to open the *Adjust Color For Skin Tone* dialog. Make sure you have the *Preview* checkbox checked so that the changes you make will be visible. Click on one person's face in the photo and Photoshop Elements adjusts the colors.

3 If you do not like the adjustment that Photoshop Elements makes, click again on another part of someone's face to sample a different skin tone. Alternately, you can fine-tune the original color adjustment using the *Tan*, *Blush*, and *Temperature* sliders in the dialog.

Adjusting the *Tan* slider adjusts the amount of brown in the skin tones and adjusting the *Blush* slider adjusts the amount of red in the skin tones. The *Temperature* slider changes the overall color of the skin tones — it makes them bluer (colder), when the slider is in the blue area and more red/orange (warmer), when the slider is in the red area.

4 The *Adjust Color For Skin Tone* tool has fixed this image so the young people look a more natural color.

Fixing a heritage photo

With a scanner and your editing software, you can scan old family photos, fix them up, and share them with others via your scrapbook. Many family photos will suffer some damage due to age and excessive handling, and you will want to fix some of this damage before scrapbooking them and sharing them.

I This old family photo has suffered some significant damage, including a rather nasty tear. With a little bit of work it can, however, be restored to its former glory.

2 Let's start with the worst damage first — this is the tear. Use the *Clone Stamp* tool (see page 46 for details of this tool) and sample a portion of the image close by the tear and paint over the damaged area with this. Continue to sample all along the tear to paint it out completely.

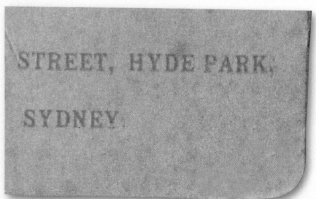

3 Use the *Zoom* tool to enlarge the image and check for other areas of damage. Move around the image using the scroll bars on the right and bottom of the image window.

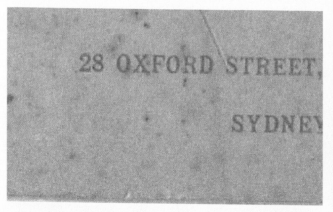

4 Where a photo has small age spots, such as those shown here, you can use the *Spot Healing Brush* tool (see page 45 for a discussion of this tool), to remove them. Longer creases like you see in the top of this image can be fixed using the *Clone Stamp* tool.

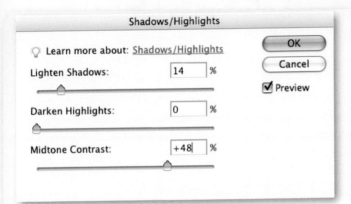

5 Now the damage is fixed, check the image for other problems. It lacks contrast and, if you look carefully, you will see that there are not a lot of very light or very dark areas in the image. To improve this, click the *Enhance* menu and choose *Adjust Lighting > Shadows/Highlights*. In this case we have lightened the shadows a little and increased the *Midtone Contrast* to bring some of the detail out of the shadows and to add some much-needed contrast to the image.

6 The image was scanned as a grayscale image — you can tell this by the image title bar which says "(Gray8)." Because it is a grayscale image, you cannot add any color to it until it is converted to a color image. To do this, click the *Image* menu and choose *Mode > RGB Color*.

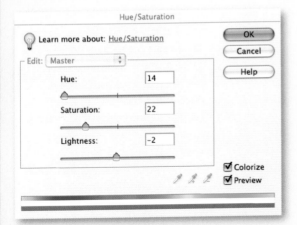

7 To add color back into the image, click the *Enhance* menu and choose *Adjust Color > Adjust Hue/Saturation*. Check the *Colorize* checkbox and the *Preview* checkbox and drag the *Hue* slider until you get approximately the desired color. Now adjust the *Saturation* and *Lightness* sliders to get the desired intensity of color. Click *OK* when you are satisfied with the result.

8 This photo now looks much better than it did. The tear is gone and a lot of the age spots have been removed. It has also been returned to the sepia color of the original image in keeping with its age.

Fun with filters

Sometimes you'll have a photograph you love but is far from perfect, and that cannot be fixed by any of the means that we have discussed so far. For example, the photo might be very blurry — but, if you love it, you'll still want to scrap it. Applying a painterly effect to the photo can hide this blurriness and give you a wonderful image fit to scrapbook.

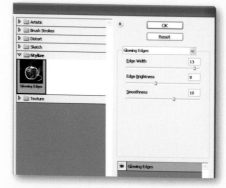

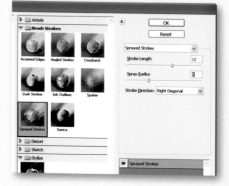

1 This photograph of a young girl is a pretty shot but it is out of focus. There's little that can be done to make it crisp and sharp, so we'll have to live with the fact that it is blurry. It's a great photo to apply a painting filter to.

2 Before applying a filter, fix the image as much as you can by adjusting any color cast, removing red eye and using the lighting tools to fix the image lightness and contrast.

3 Choose black and white as your foreground and background colors, click the *Filter* menu and choose *Filter Gallery*. This opens the *Filter Gallery* and shows your photo with various filters applied to it.

Select the *Brush Strokes* or *Artistic* group and experiment with filters from these groups. For this image, the *Sprayed Strokes* filter works particularly well. Set a *Stroke Length* of 12, a *Spray Radius* of 7, and set the *Stroke Direction* to *Right Diagonal*. Adjust the settings for your particular image to get the best possible results. When you are happy with the image, click *OK* to apply the filter to your photo.

4 The edited image now has a distinct painterly look that overcomes the problem of it being out of focus. It's a pretty image and the filter has saved it, making it perfectly suitable for use on a scrapbook page.

Tip
Some filters in the *Filter Gallery*, particularly the *Sketch* filters, use the currently selected foreground and background colors as the colors to paint on the image. Before using these filters, select a foreground and background color that you want to work with.

Color highlights

You have probably seen this effect in advertising and on gift cards. A portion of the image is highlighted in color and the remainder of the image is made black and white. It is a fun effect that, with a little bit of practice, is easy to create. Use it to add focus to the important part of your photo, particularly if the shot is very busy.

1 This image of a cello in a music store window is very bright and colorful. To draw attention to the instrument, we will leave it in color and remove the color from the remainder of the image.

2 Right/Ctrl-click the Background layer and choose *Duplicate Layer* and then click *OK*. With the Background copy layer still selected, choose *Enhance > Adjust Color > Adjust Hue/ Saturation*, drag the *Saturation* slider to -100 and click *OK*. This removes all of the color from the image.

3 Select the *Eraser* tool from the Toolbar and select a soft round brush. Set the *Opacity* to 100 percent and size the brush small enough so you can use it to erase the cello. Erase over the musical instrument (or the subject of your photo) to display the color layer below. You may need to make the brush smaller as you work around the edges of the object.

4 The finished photo shows the cello in full color with the remainder of the image in black and white. This is a fun effect that you can use in all sorts of images, and you'll find there's a bonus — black and white goes well with just about any background.

Tip

If you make a mistake while erasing the top layer, click the *Undo* button to immediately undo the brushstroke. You will get best results if you work carefully and take your time erasing the main image.

Celebrate your Uniqueness

Soar

Be Yourself

Follow your heart

Shine

Be Original

the templates and embellishments

contents

Achievement

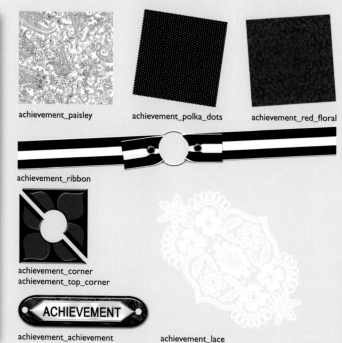

achievement_paisley

achievement_polka_dots

achievement_red_floral

achievement_ribbon

achievement_corner
achievement_top_corner

ACHIEVEMENT

achievement_achievement

achievement_lace

Baby

baby_background

baby_blue_dot_paper

baby_stripe_paper

baby_brad

baby_baby

baby_tag

baby_bottom_stitching

baby_top_stitching

Beloved pet

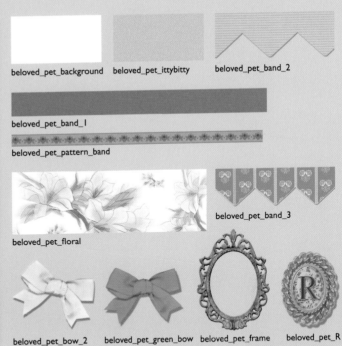

beloved_pet_background   beloved_pet_ittybitty   beloved_pet_band_2

beloved_pet_band_1

beloved_pet_pattern_band

beloved_pet_floral

beloved_pet_band_3

beloved_pet_bow_2   beloved_pet_green_bow   beloved_pet_frame   beloved_pet_R

Big kids

big_kids_background_2   big_kids_floral_button

big_kids_beads

big_kids_squiggle   big_kids_big_kids

big_kids_wave   big_kids_pattern

Boy

I have to admit that I've been shocked at just how different boys really are from little girls. Even though Cade's only 22 months old, it's already obvious that he's all boy, with all the energy and mystery that comes with it!

boy_blue_material

boy_border_2

boy_border

boy_boy

boy_rivet

boy_tag

Boy and his dog

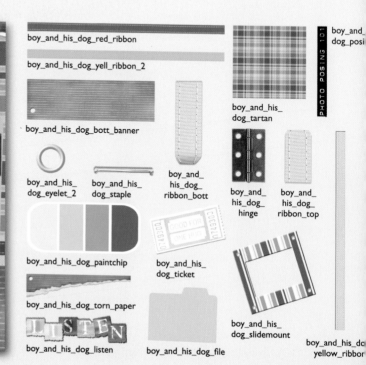

boy_and_his_dog_red_ribbon

boy_and_his_dog_yell_ribbon_2

boy_and_his_dog_bott_banner

boy_and_his_dog_eyelet_2

boy_and_his_dog_staple

boy_and_his_dog_ribbon_bott

boy_and_his_dog_tartan

boy_and_his_dog_hinge

boy_and_his_dog_ribbon_top

boy_and_his_dog_paintchip

boy_and_his_dog_ticket

boy_and_his_dog_torn_paper

boy_and_his_dog_slidemount

boy_and_his_dog_listen

boy_and_his_dog_file

boy_and_his_dog_yellow_ribbor

boy_and_his_dog_posi

Bunny boy

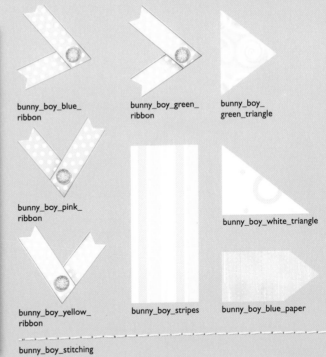

bunny_boy_blue_ribbon

bunny_boy_green_ribbon

bunny_boy_green_triangle

bunny_boy_pink_ribbon

bunny_boy_white_triangle

bunny_boy_yellow_ribbon

bunny_boy_stripes

bunny_boy_blue_paper

bunny_boy_stitching

Christmas miracle

christmas_stripes

christmas_leaves

christmas_polkadot

christmas_bells

christmas_christmas

christmas_ribbon

christmas_snowflake

christmas_snowflake3

christmas_snowflake4

Cute as a button

Ava Grace

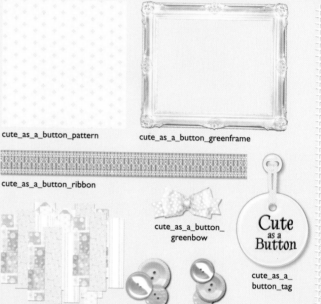

cute_as_a_button_pattern

cute_as_a_button_greenframe

cute_as_a_button_ribbon

cute_as_a_button_collage

cute_as_a_button_greenbow

cute_as_a_button_tag

cute_as_a_button_buttons

cute_as_a_button_buttons2

cute_as_a_bu stitching

Cutie patootie

CUTIE PATOOTIE

patootie - (pa-toodie) "sweetheart, pretty girl," colloquial Amer.Eng., 1921, perhaps a corruption of sweet potato.

Noelle

CUTIE

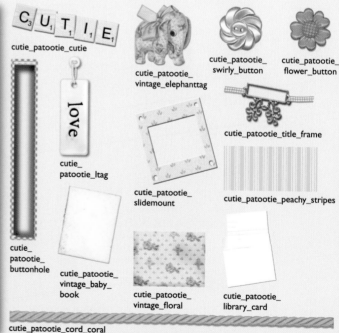

cutie_patootie_cutie

cutie_patootie_vintage_elephanttag

cutie_patootie_swirly_button

cutie_patootie_flower_button

love

cutie_patootie_ltag

cutie_patootie_title_frame

cutie_patootie_slidemount

cutie_patootie_peachy_stripes

cutie_patootie_buttonhole

cutie_patootie_vintage_baby_book

cutie_patootie_vintage_floral

cutie_patootie_library_card

cutie_patootie_cord_coral

Fairy

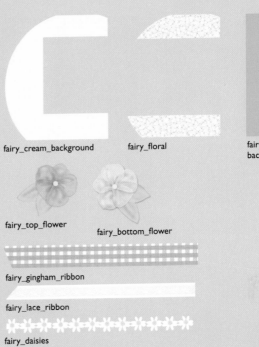

fairy_cream_background

fairy_floral

fairy_red_background

Fairy Fun

fairy_top_flower

fairy_bottom_flower

fairy_gingham_ribbon

fairy_lace_ribbon

fairy_daisies

fairy_fairy_fun

Fall

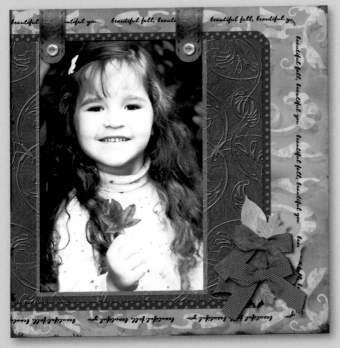

fall_strap_2   fall_strap_1

fall_inked_edge

fall_leaves_bows

fall_border_1

fall_border_2

fall_border_3

Family quilt

family_quilt_green_velvet

family_quilt_red_patch

family_quilt_red_panel

family_quilt_background

family_quilt_title

Our Family

family_quilt_red_plaid

family_quilt_star

family_quilt_wreath

family_quilt_tree

Farm

farm_red_background

farm_ribbon

farm_floral

farm_wood

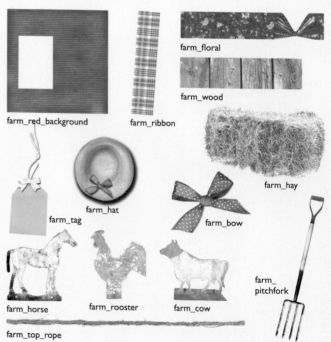

farm_tag

farm_hat

farm_bow

farm_hay

farm_horse

farm_rooster

farm_cow

farm_pitchfork

farm_top_rope

First love forever love

first_love_
background

first_love_card

first_love_ephemera

first_love_card_3

first_love_card_2

first_love_paper

first_love_letters

first_love_paper_clip

first_love_pen

first_love_blotter

first_love_
blotter_front

first_love_postcard

Flowers for mom

flowers_4u_stamps

flowers_flower

flowers_green_tag

flowers_white_tag

flowers_peach_tag

flowers_orange_paper

flowers_ribbon_frame

flowers_sunflower_paper

flowers_stripes

flowers_tag_string

Friend

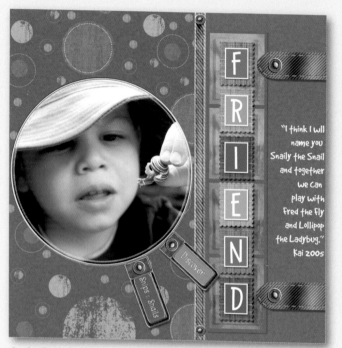

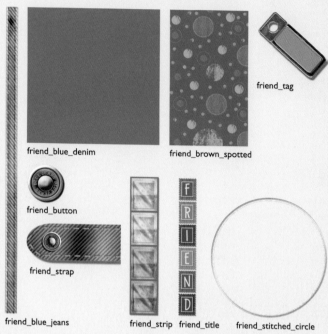

friend_blue_denim

friend_brown_spotted

friend_tag

friend_button

friend_strap

friend_blue_jeans

friend_strip

friend_title

friend_stitched_circle

Full circle

full_circle_background

full_circle_black_dots

full_circle_dots

full_circle_white_circle

full_circle_white_square

full_circle_scallop1

full_circle_bow

full_circle_scallop2

full_circle_stitch

Garden party

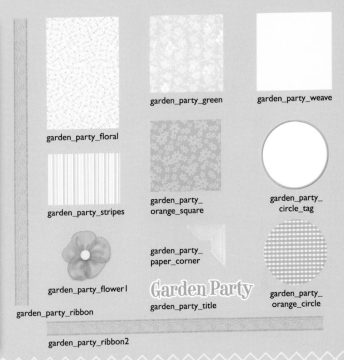

garden_party_floral

garden_party_green

garden_party_weave

garden_party_stripes

garden_party_orange_square

garden_party_circle_tag

garden_party_flower1

garden_party_paper_corner

garden_party_title

garden_party_orange_circle

garden_party_ribbon

garden_party_ribbon2

Good times

good_times_background

good_times_blue

good_times_bows

good_times_file_card

good_times_hardware

good_times_screw

good_times_ribbon

good_times_mat

good_times_buttonflower

good_times_wordplate

Grandma and friend

grandma_pin

grandma_white_
background

grandma_flowered_scrap

grandma_album

grandma_ladies1

grandma_scrap

grandma_green_scrap

grandma_green_paper

grandma_floral

grandma_flowers

grandma_black_ribbon

grandma_ribbon

Invitation to dance

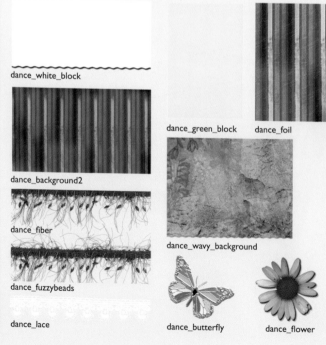

dance_white_block

dance_green_block

dance_foil

dance_background2

dance_fiber

dance_wavy_background

dance_fuzzybeads

dance_lace

dance_butterfly

dance_flower

Jingle bells

jingle_bells_decorations   jingle_bells_song

jingle_bells_title

jingle_bells_silver_frame   jingle_bells_red_snowflake   jingle_bells_background

jingle_bells_border

jingle_bells_name_plate

Joy to the world

joy_background

joy_ribbon

joy_tree

joy_clip

Just married

just_married_background

just_married_paper

just_married_brown_paper

just_married_key

just_married_frame

just_married_plate

just_married_lock

just_married_oval_tag

just_married_bow

just_married_tassle

Just us

just_us_number_2

just_us_letter_J

just_us_embossed_leaves

just_us_slidemount

just_us_letter_S

just_us_letter_U

just_us_aged_writing

just_us_ribbon_bow

just_us_soulmate_stone

just_us_letter_T

just_us_math

Lickety split

lickety_binding

lickety_title

lickety_circle_tag

lickety_blue_textured

lickety_red_polka_dots

lickety_tan_texture

lickety_monogram_L

lickety_monogram_S

lickety_stripes

lickety_corner_1
lickety_corner_2

lickety_halfcircle_2
lickety_halfcircle_1

Lil buddy

lil_buddy_alphabet

lil_buddy_patch

lil_buddy_stitching

lil_buddy_red

lil_buddy_stamp

lil_buddy_definition

lil_buddy_patch2

Loving boys

loving_boys_
background

loving_boys_floral2

loving_boys_floral

loving_boys_
tag_brad

loving_boys_frame

loving_boys_
hankerchief

loving_boys_
bow

loving_boys_locket

loving_boys_tag

loving_boys_magazine

Made with love

made_with_love_background

made_with_love_blue_swirl

made_with_
love_button

made_with_love_label

made_with_love_tag

Message from the future

If I could **speak to you from the future** I could spare you the pain of a broken heart. I could save you from the **suffering of a bad marriage** and the long hard road of raising two babies all the way to adulthood, **alone** as a single parent. I could shelter you from the tears shed for **fairweather friends** and **opportunists**. I could protect you from the **heart wrenching agony** you will feel standing at the bed of your newborn child watching him **suffer** and **struggle** to survive his first weeks of life. I could save you from every step you take into **confusion, darkness** and **despair**

I wouldn't say a thing. I wouldn't change a thing. I am who I am because of it all and I am so **incredibly blessed** with a rich and beautiful life. My only message to you is one of gratitude and the only thing I send back to you, is **love**, and the promise that it will someday all make sense. **You** are writing the story of your life and I assure you, **it is a great one.**

message_frame

message_background

message_pattern

message_message

message_pencil   message_zip   message_book   message_watch

Music

music_flower   music_turquoise   music_button

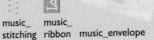

music_stitching   music_ribbon   music_envelope   music_flower2   music_tag

Passions

passions_black_floral

passions_floral_background

passions_red_floral_1

passions_vellum

passions_white_block

passions_hatpin

passions_red_floral_2

Pop's malt shop

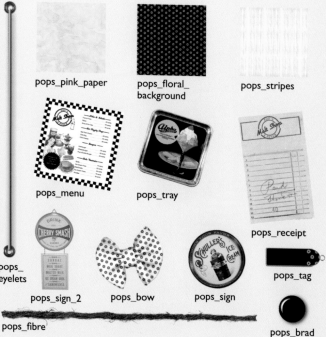

pops_pink_paper

pops_floral_background

pops_stripes

pops_menu

pops_tray

pops_receipt

pops_eyelets

pops_sign_2

pops_bow

pops_sign

pops_tag

pops_fibre

pops_brad

Pretty boy

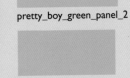
pretty_boy_background

pretty_boy_blue_background

pretty_boy_green_panel_2

pretty_boy_green_panel

pretty_boy_stripes

pretty_boy_green_ribbon

pretty_boy_train_border

pretty_boy_white_band

pretty_boy_green_brad

pretty_boy_trains

pretty_boy_train

pretty_boy_frame

pretty_boy_tag

pretty_boy_string

Princess

princess_background

princess_pink_tag

princess_tag

princess_blush

princess_green_gem

princess_pink_flower

princess_gem

princess_flower

princess_blue_flower_2

princess_blue_flower

princess_purple_gem

Promise to write

promise_background   promise_blue_floral   promise_tag1   promise_tag2

promise_inkwell   promise_letters   promise_pen   promise_frame

promise_bow   promise_postcard1

promise_ribbon   promise_telegraph

promise_ribbon2   promise_papers

promise_postcard2

promise_stitching

Read to me

read_to_me_   read_to_me_   read_to_me_   read_to_me_
argyle_2   background   stars   stripes

read_to_me_star_2   read_to_me_star

read_to_me_read

read_to_me_library_card

read_to_me_tag

read_to_me_clip   read_to_me_band

Rodeo princess

rodeo_wanted_poster

rodeo_file

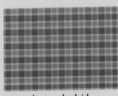
rodeo_red_plaid

rodeo_strap

rodeo_denim

rodeo_sheriff

rodeo_rope

rodeo_lace

rodeo_badge

rodeo_daisies

Senior prom

senior_prom_background

senior_prom_green

senior_prom_red

senior_prom_frame

senior_prom_
butterfly

senior_
prom_tag

senior_
prom_
leaves

senior_prom_button

senior_prom_flower

senior_prom_flowers

Star

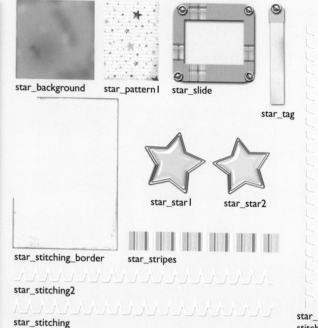

star_background

star_pattern1

star_slide

star_tag

star_star1

star_star2

star_stitching_border

star_stripes

star_stitching2

star_stitching

star_stitching3

first Sleep

This was our first night together. We had picked you up at the orphanage at about 5:00 in the afternoon and then made the three hour drive back to Kemerovo City to our hotel. We got you changed into your jammies, fed you another bottle, and then you fell asleep. We had no crib for you to sleep in, so we spent our first few nights together sharing a small twin bed. What a wonderful feeling it was though to watch you peacefully sleeping.

Stylish

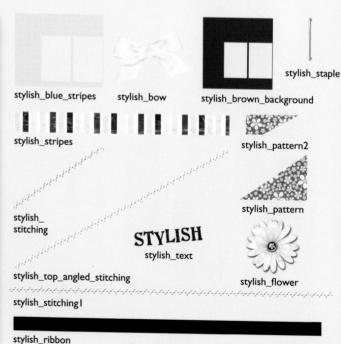

stylish_blue_stripes

stylish_bow

stylish_brown_background

stylish_staple

stylish_stripes

stylish_pattern2

stylish_stitching

stylish_pattern

stylish_top_angled_stitching

STYLISH
stylish_text

stylish_flower

stylish_stitching1

stylish_ribbon

STYLISH

This leather jacket was a gift that Mommy gave Kyla a few years back, now it's been handed down to Lydia. I think she looks adorable in it, if not a little too grown up. Often when Lydia is playing around dressing up, she asks me if she looks "STylISH". When she's wearing this cute leather jacket, she most certainly does look STylISH!

Sunrise sunset

sunrise_background

sunrise_
aqua_tile

sunrise_
tan_tile

sunrise_
3tiles

sunrise_leaf

sunrise_
blue_corner

sunrise_brn_
corner

sunrise_brown_crackle

sunrise_blue_crackle

Surfer babes

surfer_babes_
background

surfer_babes_
frame

surfer_babes_
postcard

surfer_babes_
ribbon

surfer_babes_
stamp

surfer_babes_
net_corner

surfer_babes_
net

surfer_babes_
starfish_2

surfer_babes_
starfish_3

surfer_babes_
starfish_4

surfer_babes_
starfish

surfer_babes_abes

surfer_babes_B

surfer_babes_urfer

surfer_babes_S

Too cute to spook

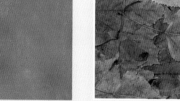

too_cute_background

too_cute_leaf_block

too_cute_
brown_panel

too_cute_red_panel

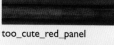

too_cute_tag

too_cute_dots

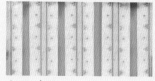

too_cute_spider

too_cute_bow

Vintage lass

vintage_lass_
background

vintage_lass_jewel

vintage_lass_
frame_salmon

vintage_lass_striped_ribbon

vintage_lass_lace_orange

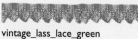

vintage_lass_lace_green

vintage_lass_pattern

vintage_lass_tag

vintage_lass_
button_salmon

vintage_lass_
jewel2

Vintage vows

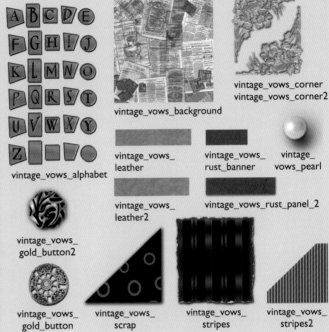

vintage_vows_alphabet

vintage_vows_background

vintage_vows_corner
vintage_vows_corner2

vintage_vows_leather

vintage_vows_rust_banner

vintage_vows_pearl

vintage_vows_leather2

vintage_vows_rust_panel_2

vintage_vows_gold_button2

vintage_vows_gold_button

vintage_vows_scrap

vintage_vows_stripes

vintage_vows_stripes2

Weathered treasures

weathered_corner

weathered_brad

weathered_key

weathered_map

weathered_corner_2

weathered_screw

weathered_brown_paper

weathered_hinge

weathered_paper

weathered_ink_edge

weathered_post_tag

weathered_strip_1

weathered_strip_2

weathered_rope

weathered_rope_2

Woman in love

In our early years together there was no digital camera so there are much fewer photos, and even fewer still of the two of us together. However, this photo of me really captures the essence of that time because it is very dear to me that this is the face of a woman in love.

THIS IS THE FACE OF A WOMAN IN LOVE

I am 37 years old here and I am nearly as pretty as the day I turned sixteen

That is because the person whom I am looking at is you.

This is the face of the woman who adores you

You are the glow on my cheeks, the twinkle in my eye, the fire in my heart the love that brings my soul out to play You are my reason for being and my reason for wanting to fully blossom.

1999

woman_background

woman_arrow2

THIS IS THE FACE OF THE WOMAN WHO ADORES YOU
woman_text2

woman_arrow

woman_blue_doodles

woman_pointer

woman_flower

THIS IS THE FACE OF A WOMAN IN LOVE
woman_text1

woman_pink_doodles

Young love

My greatest wish for all of my children is that their lives are filled with love. May you always love and be loved, cherish and be totally adored in return

Young Love

Dan & Courtney

young_love_background

young_love_white_panel

young_love_heart

young_love_text

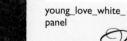

young_love_frame

young_love_tag

young_love_stitching

Assorted embellishments

You can use these additional embellishments to create your own scrapbook page designs. To select a single element, such as a letter, from an image, first draw around it with one of the *Marquee* tools. Next, switch to the *Move* tool and drag the selected element into your page.

alpha_flower_A_LC

alpha_flower_B_LC

alpha_flower_C_LC

alpha_flower_D_LC

alpha_flower_E_LC

alpha_flower_F_LC

alpha_flower_G_LC

alpha_flower_H_LC

alpha_flower_I_LC

alpha_flower_J_LC

alpha_flower_K_LC

alpha_flower_L_LC

alpha_flower_M_LC

alpha_flower_N_LC

alpha_flower_O_LC

alpha_flower_P_LC

alpha_flower_Q_LC

alpha_flower_R_LC

alpha_flower_S_LC

alpha_flower_T_LC

alpha_flower_U_LC

alpha_flower_V_LC

alpha_flower_W_LC

alpha_flower_X_LC

alpha_flower_Y_LC

alpha_flower_Z_LC

alpha_flower_A_UC

alpha_flower_B_UC

alpha_flower_C_UC

alpha_flower_D_UC

alpha_flower_E_UC

alpha_flower_F_UC

alpha_flower_G_UC

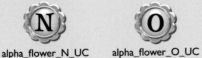
alpha_flower_H_UC

alpha_flower_I-UC

alpha_flower_J_UC

alpha_flower_K_UC

alpha_flower_L_UC

alpha_flower_M_UC

alpha_flower_N_UC

alpha_flower_O_UC

alpha_flower_P_UC

alpha_flower_Q_UC

alpha_flower_R_UC

alpha_flower_S_UC

alpha_flower_T_UC

alpha_flower_U_UC

alpha_flower_V_UC

alpha_flower_W_UC

alpha_flower_X_UC

alpha_flower_Y_UC

alpha_flower_Z_UC

alpha_flower_!

alpha_flower_?

alpha_flower_Aunt

alpha_flower_girl

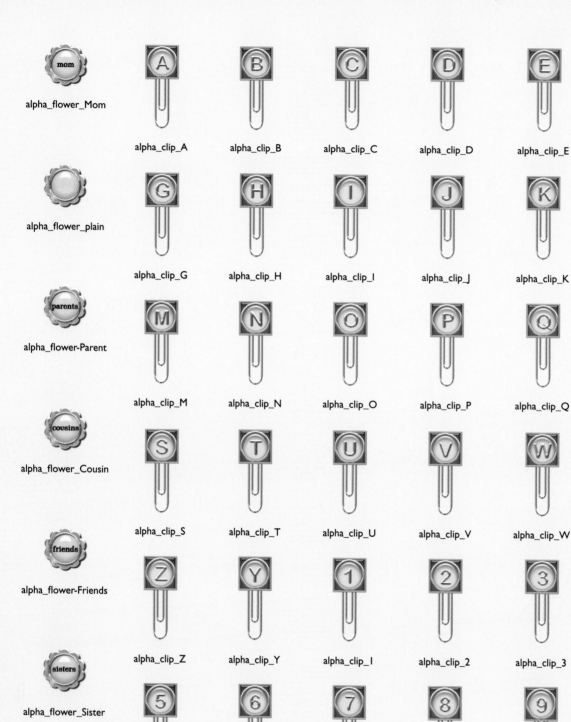

alpha_flower_Mom

alpha_clip_A | alpha_clip_B | alpha_clip_C | alpha_clip_D | alpha_clip_E | alpha_clip_F

alpha_flower_plain

alpha_clip_G | alpha_clip_H | alpha_clip_I | alpha_clip_J | alpha_clip_K | alpha_clip_L

alpha_flower-Parent

alpha_clip_M | alpha_clip_N | alpha_clip_O | alpha_clip_P | alpha_clip_Q | alpha_clip_R

alpha_flower_Cousin

alpha_clip_S | alpha_clip_T | alpha_clip_U | alpha_clip_V | alpha_clip_W | alpha_clip_X

alpha_flower-Friends

alpha_clip_Z | alpha_clip_Y | alpha_clip_I | alpha_clip_2 | alpha_clip_3 | alpha_clip_4

alpha_flower_Sister

alpha_clip_5 | alpha_clip_6 | alpha_clip_7 | alpha_clip_8 | alpha_clip_9 | alpha_clip_Plain

alpha_mapcaps_A

 alpha_mapcaps_B

 alpha_mapcaps_C

 alpha_mapcaps_D

 alpha_mapcaps_E

 alpha_mapcaps_F

 alpha_mapcaps_G

 alpha_mapcaps_H

 alpha_mapcaps_I

 alpha_mapcaps_J

 alpha_mapcaps_K

 alpha_mapcaps_L

 alpha_mapcaps_M

 alpha_mapcaps_N

 alpha_mapcaps_O

 alpha_mapcaps_P

 alpha_mapcaps_Q

 alpha_mapcaps_R

 alpha_mapcaps_S

 alpha_mapcaps_T

 alpha_mapcaps_U

 alpha_mapcaps_V

 alpha_mapcaps_W

 alpha_mapcaps_X

 alpha_mapcaps_Y

 alpha_mapcaps_Z

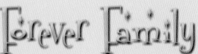 titles_forever_family

 titles_family_reunion

 titles_family_ties

 titles_patchwork_family

 titles_family_fun

spring_metal_letters_A

spring_metal_letters_B

spring_metal_letters_C

spring_metal_letters_D

spring_metal_letters_E

spring_metal_letters_F

spring_metal_letters_G

spring_metal_letters_H

spring_metal_letters_I

spring_metal_letters_J

spring_metal_letters_K

spring_metal_letters_L

spring_metal_letters_M

spring_metal_letters_N

spring_metal_letters_O

spring_metal_letters_P

butterflies_stainedgl

spring_metal_letters_Q

spring_metal_letters_R

spring_metal_letters_S

spring_metal_letters_T

spring_metal_letters_U

spring_metal_letters_V

spring_metal_letters_W

spring_metal_letters_X

spring_metal_letters_Y

spring_metal_letters_Z

spring_metal_letters_-

floral_eyelets

pjcaps

pinback_buttons

tags_pjex_green_bow   tags_pjex_pink_bow

flowers_family_yellow   flowers_family_white1   flowers_family_purple

spiralsandflowers   flowers_family_pink   flowers_family_orange   flowers_family_lightpurp1

 american_flag_a

 american_flag_b

 american_flag_c

 american_flag_d

 american_flag_e

 american_flag_f

 american_flag_g

 american_flag_h

 american_flag_i

 american_flag_j

 american_flag_k

 american_flag_l

 american_flag_m

 american_flag_n

 american_flag_o

 american_flag_p

 american_flag_q

 american_flag_r

 american_flag_s

 american_flag_t

 american_flag_u

 american_flag_v

 american_flag_w

 american_flag_x

 american_flag_y

 american_flag_z

 american_flag_0

 american_flag_1

 american_flag_2

 american_flag_3

 american_flag_4

american_flag_5

american_flag_6

american_flag_7

american_flag_8

american_flag_9

Husband Wife Myself Mother
Nana Papa Daughter Father
Girlfriend Partner Son Aunt Uncle
Boyfriend Pet Grandmother
Beloved Great Grandfather Sister
Dog Cat Brother Friend Cousin

familymembers2

familymembers1

Grandson Nephew
Granddaughter Niece
Inlaw Step God
GodMother Fiancé
GodFather Child
Half Twin

familymembers3

decoclips

GROW

LOVE

SPRING

HAPPY

SUNNY

FRESH

INSPIRE

MOM

EASTER

BLOOM

SWEET

springtrinkitz_words_maya

0 1 2 3 4 5 6 7 8 9

spring_metalnumbers_maya

button_ohoh

cord_charcoal_maya

screws

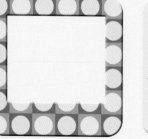

slidemount_oddmod

Cute as a Button

Pretty in Pink

Princess

Sweet

My Girl

Happy

Imagine

Dream come True

Look at Me!

Peek -a- Boo

Adorable

Sweet Prince

My Boy

Little Man

Tiny Toes

jellytags_baby_maya

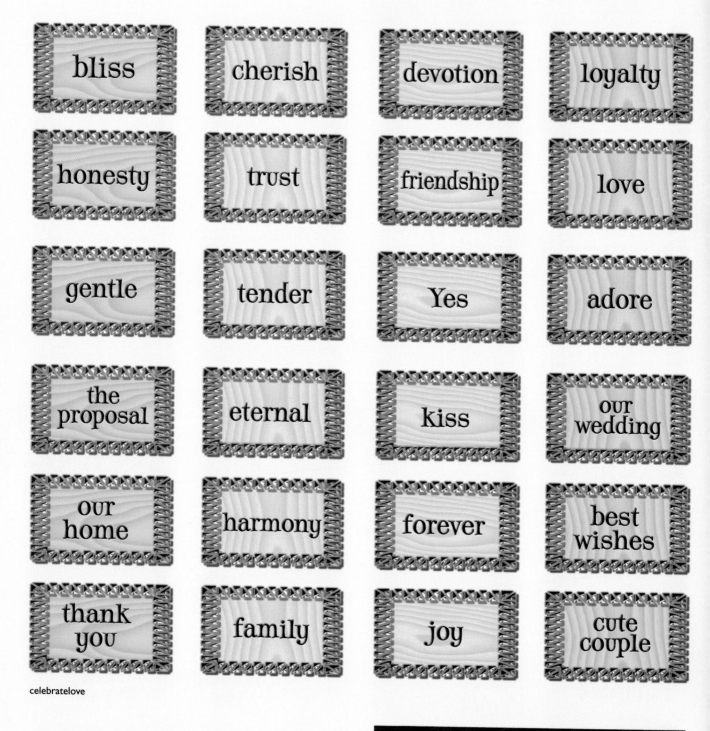

bliss	cherish	devotion	loyalty
honesty	trust	friendship	love
gentle	tender	Yes	adore
the proposal	eternal	kiss	our wedding
our home	harmony	forever	best wishes
thank you	family	joy	cute couple

celebratelove

chainborder

chainonleather_maya

frames_birthday

butterflybead_wordch_girl

butterflybead_wordch_kisses

spring_trinkitz_flowers_1

spring_trinkitz_flowers_2

butterflybead_wordch_love

butterflybead_wordch_sweet

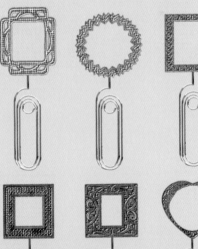

titles_family_picnic

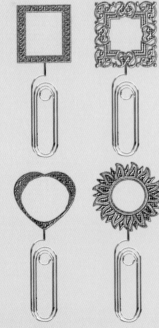

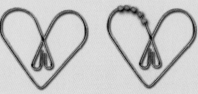 

clips_heartsandbeads

clippers_fancyframes

postagestamps

christmastgift-
tags_seasonsg

christmastgifttags_
merrychrist2

christmastgifttags_
merrychrist

christmastgift-
tags_happyh

christmastgifttags_
happyh2

christmastgift-
tags_ourhouse

journalcards_maya_orange

tags_candy_blank

funkytags_maya

twillblank

ribbon_blackplaid_maya

riseandshinejell

WISH SOFT GROW HOME SHINE

HAPPY FLIRT FROLIC

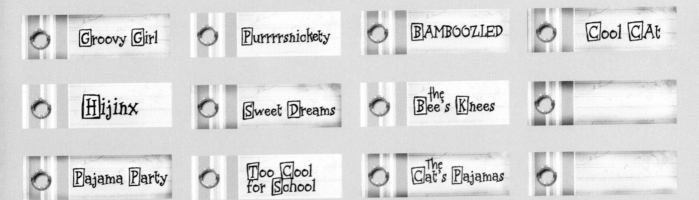

Groovy Girl   Purrrrsnickety   BAMBOOZLED   Cool CAt

Hijinx   Sweet Dreams   the Bee's Knees

Pajama Party   Too Cool for School   The Cat's Pajamas

tags_pjexpressions

Glossary

Background color A color that will be used when an eraser is applied to a background layer in an image or that is used when a piece is cut from a background layer. The background color appears with the foreground color in a box at the foot of the Toolbar.

Brush The digital equivalent of a regular paint brush that can not only paint onto an image but also be used to erase areas of the image.

Constrain proportions A feature that fixes the ratio between the width and height of an image and used when resizing it to ensure the image remains in proportion and is not stretched or squashed.

Default The settings that will take effect if you do not make a change to them.

Download To move files, images, fonts or programs from one computer or device to another. Typically you download from the internet and upload onto it. Until you download files such as fonts, you can't use them on your computer.

DPI Dots Per Inch — see PPI

Embellishments Additional objects on a scrapbook page added for decorative effect. May include ribbons, buckles, tags, and flowers.

Eyedropper tool Can be used when selecting a color to use and allows you to sample a color from an image. This tool is useful when matching a color for text with colors in the image

Filter A process applied to an image that changes or distorts it. For example, a blur effect removes some of the focus from the image, and a watercolor effect makes the photo look as if it has been painted. Effects are generally customizable, so you can apply the amount of the effect you want to apply to a given image.

Font A series of characters all drawn in a similar style, typically including A-Z, a-z, 0-9, and punctuation. These are stored in a file on your computer and, when you can select a font to use, the characters appear drawn in that style. Fonts must be installed before they can be used.

Foreground color The color that is used by the Brush tool to paint with. The foreground and background colors appear in boxes at the foot of the Toolbar. See also Background color.

Hue Pure spectrum colors such as red, orange, yellow, green, blue, and purple. In Photoshop Elements the Hue adjuster is a horizontal slider that can be moved from Red (at 0) through Yellow to Green, Blue and then Purple, and back to Red again at value 360.

Journaling Text displayed on a scrapbook page that describes the photos on the page or the story behind them.

Layer A level in an image. Layers are managed in the Layers palette and each layer can contain a portion of an image. Image data on the top layers block out image data on layers below.

LCD Liquid Crystal Display — a small screen on the back of a digital camera that can be used to frame your photos and to view a photo when you have taken it. In general, the LCD screen is a better choice for previewing a photo than using the viewfinder.

Marquee The shape around an object that appears when you Ctrl/Cmd-click on its layer or that you see when you choose one of the two Marquee tools. The marquee is often referred to as "marching ants" and shows the area you are working on.

Opacity A measure of the layer's transparency, i.e. how much you can see through it. If Opacity is 100% the layer is not transparent, if it is 0% opacity it is fully transparent. From 0 to 100% opacity the layer becomes increasingly less transparent and more opaque.

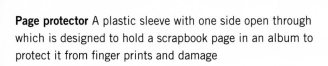

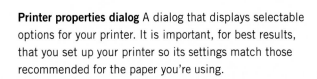

Page protector A plastic sleeve with one side open through which is designed to hold a scrapbook page in an album to protect it from finger prints and damage

Paper type The kind of paper used for a print job. Setting the paper type correctly is important because different papers absorb different amounts of ink. Shiny paper absorbs less ink, so selecting the correct paper type ensures best printing results.

Photo mat A small digital paper image that you can set behind a photo that extends a small distance beyond its edges and separates it from the page background.

Polarizing filter A round glass filter that screws onto a camera lens or sits in a special filter rack in front of the lens. The filter reduces reflections and glare so skies are darker. The filter's effect can be adjusted by rotating it.

PPI Pixels Per Inch — a measure of resolution in printing and scanning. A 72 ppi scan, suited for screen display, will scan 72 points per inch in each direction giving 72 x 72 pixels. For printing, scanning at 300 ppi is required for 300 ppi printing.

Print quality A measure of the quality of the printout — at low quality, less dots per inch of ink are printed on the paper, less ink is used and the final image is not as well defined or as saturated as it might be. At high quality maximum dots per inch are printed, printing is slower but generally the result is a more detailed, colorful result.

Print size The size of the printed image on the page. This is the same as or smaller than the paper size. Some printers can print borderless on certain paper sizes and, in this case, the print size will be the same as the paper size. For older printers, the print size will be smaller than the paper size to allow for the border area where the printer can't print.

Printer properties dialog A dialog that displays selectable options for your printer. It is important, for best results, that you set up your printer so its settings match those recommended for the paper you're using.

Rotate To swivel an image around a central axis so edges that were horizontal and vertical are now at an angle.

Saturation A measure of the intensity of a color or colors in an image. At high saturation the colors are bright and deep and at low saturation they are muted and gray.

Slide show A visual display of photos one at a time on a computer screen or TV often displaying special transitions between the individual photos and can be combined with music and narrative.

SLR Single Lens Reflex — these cameras generally have interchangeable lenses and when you line-up the picture you preview it through the same lens that takes the photo. This gives you better control over framing the photo and focusing it.

Title A heading on a scrapbook page that sets the scene for the page and introduces it to the viewer.

VCD Video Compact Disk — a CD written using a format that allows movies or slide shows to be played in a regular DVD player — its an option for use if you don't have a DVD burner.

Resources

Font sites
onescrappysite.com
scrapvillage.com/fonts.htm
momscorner4kids.com/fonts/index.htm
1001fonts.com
fontgarden.com
creativespirits.net/graphics/
dafont.com/en/

Photo sharing sites
flickr.com
photobucket.com
bubbleshare.com
photos.yahoo.com

Blog sites
blogger.com
typepad.com
sixapart.com
wordpress.com

Scrapbook communities
digiscrapdivas.com
digitalscrapbookplace.com
scrapbook-bytes.com
scrapbookgraphics.com
twopeasinabucket.com

Slide show software
Microsoft Photo Story 3 for Windows XP
microsoft.com/downloads/details.aspx?
FamilyID=92755126-a008-49b3-b3f4-
6f33852af9c1&DisplayLang=en

iPhoto for Mac
apple.com/ilife/iphoto/

DVD burning
iDVD for Mac — apple.com/ilife/idvd/
MyDVD for the PC — sonic.com
Nero PhotoShow Deluxe — nero.com

Acknowledgments

Thank you
Writing a book like this is a team effort and I've been blessed with working with a wonderful selection of art from Maya, thank you! To Michelle Shefveland from CottageArts.net who is always so supportive and encouraging, thank you. To Tom Mugridge and Ben Renow-Clarke at Ilex Press, it is wonderful to work with you again, and thank you for all your hard work in getting this book to press. Finally, heartfelt thanks to Michelle Zimmerman and my cat Molly who keep the home fires burning and allow me the space to focus on my art and writing.

Thanks also to
Lori and Tim, Allison, Ginger, Katyann; Heather, Brandi and Casey; Jim and Pam Deflinger; and Diana Brélaz, for the use of personal photos.

Dedication
To my parents Diana and John Brélaz.

Supplies
Thank you to these companies for their assistance in materials: Bazzill Basics, SEI, K & Company, 7 Gypsies, Hewlett Packard

Photo credits
Jim Derflinger, Brenda Smith, Frank Vallin, Michelle Zimmerman, Helen Bradley

All template and embellishment files copyright Maya (Janice Dye-Szucs) except: Baby, Boy, Fairy, Fall, Farm, Star, Stylish — copyright Jodi Perry; and Full circle, Garden party, Good times, Grandma and friend, Invitation to dance, Lil buddy, Loving boys, Passions, Pop's malt shop, Pretty boy, Promise to write, Vintage vows, Weathered treasures — copyright Ruth Anne McQuillin.